WOMAN'S OWN

SOUPS, STARTERS & SNACKS

SOUPS, STARTERS & SNACKS

Classic step-by-step Cookery Collection

GINA STEER

COOKERY EDITOR OF WOMAN'S OWN

HAMLYN

CONTENTS

SOUPS 6

STARTERS 30

SNACKS 58

First published 1992
Hamlyn is an imprint of
Octopus Illustrated Publishing,
part of Reed International Books Limited,
Michelin House, 81 Fulham Road,
London, SW3 6RB

A catalogue record for this book is
available from the British Library

ISBN 0 600 57567 5

Produced by Mandarin Offset
Printed and Bound in Hong Kong

NOTES

Both metric and imperial measurements have been used in all recipes.
Use one set of measurements only and not a mixture of both.

Standard level spoon measurements are used in all recipes
1 tablespoon = one 15 ml spoon
1 teaspoon = one 5 ml spoon

Ovens should be preheated to the specific temperature.
If using a fan assisted oven, follow manufacturer's instructions
for adjusting the temperature.

Learn how to cook delicious and attractive dishes in next to no time with these Classic Step-by-Step Cookery Books. It has been said that if you can read you can cook and these books aim to prove that this really is true.

As a mum with two daughters, I was most concerned to discover just how little cooking is taught in schools and it became apparent that many of our basic recipes and skills were in danger of being forgotten. So Woman's Own decided to publish one recipe each week with clear instructions plus easy to follow colour steps which illustrated the various skills and techniques involved.

We have now brought together these recipes into a series of cookery books and in this volume we have put together 45 stunning recipes for you to cook and enjoy.

There's chilled Gazpacho Soup, a colourful and impressive starter for a dinner party; a Lentil Soup that'll keep the whole family warm and glowing. There are pâtés, terrines and mousses, ideal for either formal or informal occasions. Delicious fish and shellfish recipes such as Fish Cakes or Dressed Crab.

If you want a hearty and easy snack, how about meatballs with tasty tangy sauce, or a Pasty Then if you've a vegetarian in the family, there's Cheese Soufflé, Onion Tart and loads more.

All the recipes have been thoroughly tested in the Woman's Own Test Kitchen to ensure a perfect result every time. So you know that which ever recipe you decide to cook, it really will work and you've got the step-by-step pictures to help as well. I guarantee that each recipe will taste every bit as good as it looks.

I hope you enjoy the book.

Happy cooking

Gina Steer

WINTER LENTIL SOUP

Hearty and warming, this delicious soup contains all the ingredients needed to keep everyone warm and glowing during the cold winter months. Serve it with chunks of crusty brown bread.

4 oz/100 g red lentils

2 small onions

2 bay leaves

1 medium carrot

4 oz/100 g swede

4 oz/100 g turnips

6 oz/175 g leeks

6 oz/175 g ripe tomatoes

3 oz/75 g streaky bacon

2 tbsp oil

6 oz/175 g ripe tomatoes

¾ pint/450 ml vegetable stock

1-2 tbsp tomato purée

grated rind and juice
    1 small orange

salt and freshly ground
    black pepper

1 tbsp freshly chopped parsley

Wash the lentils thoroughly. Bring a pan of water to the boil then add the lentils. Peel the onions and chop one, then add to the pan with the bay leaves. Bring the pan to the boil, cover, reduce the heat then simmer for 30 mins or until the lentils are soft. Drain then discard the bay leaves. Meanwhile prepare the remaining vegetables. Peel the carrot, swede and turnip then cut into small dice. Wash and trim the leeks and slice. Make a small cross in the top of each tomato, place in a bowl, cover with boiling water, leave for 5 mins then drain. Peel the tomatoes discarding the core and seeds if preferred. Chop remaining onion.

Trim the bacon discarding the rind and cartilage, then cut or chop into small pieces. Heat the oil in a large pan then gently sauté the prepared onion and bacon for 5-8 mins or until they are softened.

Add the remaining vegetables except for the tomatoes and continue to sauté gently for a further 5 mins. Pour in the

HANDY TIP

If preferred, the soup can be passed through a food processor or liquidizer and blended until smooth. Add a little extra stock to help in the blending. Reheat.

stock and add the drained lentils.

Blend the tomato purée with 2 tbsp of water and stir into the pan together with the grated rind and juice of the orange. Bring the contents of the pan to the boil, cover the pan and reduce the heat and allow the soup to simmer gently for 25-30 mins or until the vegetables are soft. Stir in the chopped tomatoes with seasoning to taste and continue to cook for a further 10 mins. Adjust seasoning, sprinkle with the freshly chopped parsley then serve immediately with crusty bread.

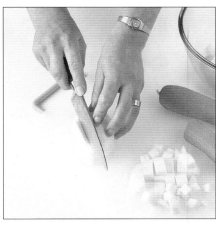

1. Add the lentils to a pan of boiling water with 1 chopped onion and bay leaves

2. Peel the vegetables then slice the leeks and dice the turnip and carrots

3. Dice the swede and remaining onion. Cover the tomatoes with boiling water, leave for 2 mins, drain and peel

4. Heat the oil in a pan then gently sauté the chopped bacon and onion for 5-8 mins or until soft and transparent

5. Add the prepared vegetables then continue to sauté for a further 5 mins, stirring occasionally

6. Add the stock to the pan then the drained lentils. Blend the tomato purée with 2 tbsp of water and add to pan

MINESTRONE SOUP

It's everybody's favourite... minestrone, with its wonderful rich tomato flavour. Packed full of tasty vegetables and with a sprinkling of Parmesan cheese on top, it's a meal in itself – enough to satisfy the heartiest appetite.

Calories per portion: 208 **SERVES 6**

1 onion

2 garlic cloves

1 leek

2 celery sticks

1 carrot

1 turnip

1 large potato

4 medium tomatoes

1 oz/25 g butter or margarine

2 tbsp olive oil

2 bay leaves

2 pints/1.2 litres vegetable stock

2 oz/50 g pasta twists

2 tbsp tomato purée

salt and freshly ground
   black pepper

3 oz/75 g green cabbage

3 slices back bacon

grated Parmesan cheese

Peel the onion, leaving the root on. Make cuts in both directions across the onion then cut down through the onion. Peel and crush the garlic cloves. Trim leek, wash thoroughly under cold water, cut into rings. Trim then wash or scrub celery, slice thinly. Peel carrot, turnip and potato, then dice.

Cut a small cross on the top of the tomatoes, place in bowl and cover with boiling water. Leave for 2 mins, drain then peel, cut into quarters and scoop out seeds. Chop flesh. Reserve all prepared vegetables.

Melt the fat with the oil in a large pan and fry the onion, garlic, leek, celery and bay leaves for 5 mins until softened. Add the stock, bring to the boil, reduce heat and simmer for 10 mins, then add the remaining diced root vegetables with the pasta twists. Continue to simmer for 10-15 mins or until almost cooked. Blend the tomato purée with 2 tbsp cold water, and stir into pan with seasoning to taste.

Wash cabbage thoroughly, drain and discard centre stalk, then shred. Remove the rind from the bacon, slice, then gently fry in a non-stick frying pan until lightly cooked. Add the chopped tomatoes, shredded cabbage and bacon to the soup and cook for a further 5-10 mins. Discard the bay leaves, adjust the seasoning and serve with grated Parmesan cheese and fresh brown bread.

If you wish to make the soup in advance, make as above but don't add cabbage and bacon. Cool quickly and store, covered, in fridge. Just before eating reheat then add cabbage. Fry bacon, stir in and serve.

HANDY TIP

Parmesan cheese has been made in Italy since before the time of the Romans. It is a cows' milk cheese and is used for grating when it is 2-4 years old. It is only made between the months of April and November. Fully mature Parmesan has a dark yellow, grainy texture and its rind is a dark brown. It has a sharp, fruity texture and is best if bought as a piece and grated just before use.

1. Peel onion and garlic, trim leek and cut into rings. Trim celery and slice

2. Make a cross in tomatoes, cover with boiling water, drain, peel and deseed

3. Melt fat with oil in a pan. Fry onion, garlic, leek and celery with bay leaves

4. Once the vegetables are softened, pour in the stock and bring to the boil

5. After simmering stock for 10 mins, add the remaining root vegetables

6. Fry the chopped bacon in a non-stick frying pan, until lightly cooked

CARROT SOUP

This is a super soup, made with fresh carrots and onion, flavoured with basil and fruity oranges, and topped with a swirl of cream. Serve it as a tasty starter or lunch-time snack – it's so easy to make when you follow this step-by-step recipe.

Calories per portion: 142

SERVES 4

I large onion

I lb/450 g carrots

2 tbsp olive oil

1½ pints/900 ml vegetable stock

few fresh basil sprigs

2 large oranges

salt and freshly ground
   black pepper

I level tsp ground mace

I level tbsp single cream

Peel and finely chop the onion. Peel and slice the carrots. Heat the olive oil in a large pan, then sauté the onion and carrots for 5 mins, or until the vegetables have softened slightly and the onion is transparent. Stir in the vegetable stock, together with one or two basil sprigs, which have been bruised slightly (reserve a couple of basil sprigs to garnish the soup).

Bring the soup to the boil, cover, then reduce for 30 mins or until the carrots are tender.

Meanwhile, prepare the orange zest for the garnish. Scrub and dry one orange, then, using a zester, pull firmly at an angle down the side of the orange so that the rind is removed in long thin strips without any of the bitter white pith beneath (this rind is always referred to as the zest).

Place the zest in a bowl and cover with boiling water. Leave to stand for at least 5 mins, before draining. Refresh in cold water. Leave to one side until required for garnishing soup.

Finely grate the rind from remaining orange and squeeze juice from both of the oranges. When carrots are cooked, remove pan from heat and discard the basil sprigs. Allow carrot mixture to cool, then place in a food processor or liquidizer. Blend to a smooth purée.

Rinse the pan and return soup to it, then stir in the grated orange rind (an easy way to remove the rind from the grater is to use a pastry brush). Season to taste with salt, freshly ground black pepper and mace.

Return the pan to the heat, then add the orange juice through a strainer. Cook gently, stirring occasionally, until piping hot. Pour soup into a warmed tureen, then swirl in the single cream.

HANDY TIP

During the summer, try serving this soup chilled as a delicious starter for a dinner party. Remember to add the cream and garnish after chilling.

Strain the prepared orange zest and use to garnish the soup, together with the remaining basil sprigs. For special occasions, serve with extra cream.

1. Heat the oil in a large pan, then sauté the chopped onion and sliced carrot for 5 mins or until softened slightly

2. Add the vegetable stock with one or two basil sprigs to the pan, then bring to the boil, cover and simmer

3. Scrub and dry one of the oranges, then, using a zester, carefully remove the rind in long thin strips

4. Discard basil sprigs, place the cooled carrot mixture in a food processor or liquidizer and blend to a smooth purée

5. Return soup to the rinsed pan and add the grated rind from the remaining orange together with seasoning

6. Return pan to the heat. Add orange juice through a strainer. Cook gently, stirring occasionally, until hot, then serve

CREAM OF TOMATO SOUP

Give everyone a delicious treat with this all-time favourite. Made from the finest of ingredients – plump tomtoes, onions and garlic, with a hint of fresh basil – it's really easy to prepare.

Calories per portion: 238

SERVES 4

1½ lb/675 g ripe tomatoes,
  washed
2 garlic cloves
1 large onion
2 sticks celery
4 oz/100 g back bacon
2 tbsp vegetable oil
few basil sprigs
¾ pint/450 ml vegetable stock
salt and freshly ground
  black pepper
2-3 tbsp tomato purée
1 tbsp cornflour
¼ pint/150 ml single cream or
  low-fat fromage frais
extra basil sprigs to garnish

Make a small cross at the stalk end of each tomato. Place in a large bowl and cover with boiling water. Leave for 2 mins then drain, peel and discard the skins. Cut tomatoes into quarters, discard the core then, using a teaspoon, scoop out the seeds and discard.

Peel and crush the garlic. Peel and finely chop the onion. Wash and trim celery and chop finely. Discard any rind from bacon, then snip into pieces with kitchen scissors. Place garlic, onion, celery and bacon, in a large saucepan with oil and fry gently for 5 mins, or

until onion is soft and transparent.

Add the prepared tomatoes and a few basil sprigs and cook gently for a further 5 mins. Pour in the stock and season with the salt and pepper. Bring to the boil, cover, then simmer gently for 15 mins, or until the tomatoes are pulpy and the vegetables are soft.

Allow to cool for 5 mins, then pass through a blender or food processor to form a purée. If a smoother soup is required, rub through a sieve and return to the rinsed pan.

Blend the tomato purée with 2 tbsp cold water and stir into the pan. Bring to just below boiling point. Blend the cornflour with 2-3 tbsp of cold water to form a smooth paste, and stir into the soup. Cook, stirring throughout with a wooden spoon, until the soup thickens slightly. Adjust the seasoning if necessary.

To serve, pour soup into a warm tureen and swirl in a little cream or fromage frais. Garnish the top with the rest of the basil sprigs. Serve remaining cream or fromage frais separately.

If preferred, allow the soup to cool slightly (for about 2 mins) then stir in all of the cream or fromage frais and serve immediately with chunks of fresh bread.

HANDY TIP

For a real indulgence, stir 2-3 tbsp of port into the soup before adding the cream. Served chilled, this makes a perfect starter for a buffet lunch.

1. Cover tomatoes with boiling water, leave for 2 mins, drain well, then skin

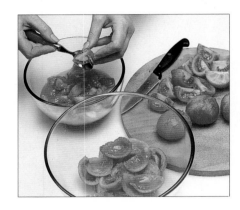

2. Cut peeled tomatoes into quarters, then scoop out seeds and discard

3. Crush garlic, peel and chop onion and wash, trim and chop celery finely; snip bacon into pieces and place in pan

4. Fry bacon, garlic, onion and celery in a large saucepan with oil for 5 mins, or until onion is soft and transparent

5. Add quartered tomatoes to the pan and cook gently for a further 5 mins, stir occasionally with a wooden spoon

6. Add a few basil sprigs to the pan, pour in the stock and bring to the boil. Cover then simmer gently for 15 mins

POTATO AND LEEK SOUP

What could be more warming on a cold, winter's day than a nourishing bowl of steaming hot potato and leek soup? Its creamy texture makes it ideal any time, – as a satisfying snack or delicious starter.

Calories per portion: 385 **SERVES 4**

1 lb/450 g potatoes
1 large onion
1 lb/450 g leeks
2 oz/50 g butter or margarine
2 bay leaves
1 pint/600 ml vegetable stock
salt and freshly ground
   black pepper
¼ pint/150 ml milk
¼ pint/150 ml single cream
½-1 tsp grated nutmeg

HANDY TIPS

Serve hot, garnished with a few blanched leek rings. When preparing leeks, reserve a few slices that are very pale green. Just before serving the soup, pour boiling water over them, leave for 2 mins, drain, then use as a garnish. Serve the soup with crusty wholemeal bread as a snack or with sliced brown bread as a starter. In the summer this soup is delicious if served chilled. It is then known as Vichyssoise. Make exactly as above except for the garnish and chill. Just before serving, stir, check seasoning then pour into a soup tureen or bowls.

Peel the potatoes and dice into ½ in/1.25 cm cubes. Peel and chop the onion. Trim the leeks, discarding the root and very green part of the leek. (This part can be used for flavouring stocks and casseroles.) Slit the leeks down the centre from top to tail, then wash under plenty of cold running water to remove any dirt or grit. Drain well then slice into 1 in/2.5 cm rings.

Melt the butter or margarine in a large pan then sauté the diced potatoes and chopped onion with the bay leaves for 5 mins. Add the sliced leeks to the pan and continue to sauté for a further 3-4 mins.

Pour in the stock, then add salt and pepper to taste. Bring to the boil, then cover with a lid and simmer for 15 mins or until the potatoes are cooked.

Remove from the heat and reserve one third of the cooked vegetables. Discard the bay leaves. Pass the remainder of the vegetables and stock through a food processor or liquidizer and blend until smooth. If you do not have either of these in your kitchen, mash well with a potato masher then rub through a fine sieve.

Return purée to a clean pan and adjust seasoning to taste, then stir in the milk, cream and nutmeg to taste. Add the reserved cooked vegetables then reheat gently, stirring occasionally with a wooden spoon. Do not allow the soup to boil otherwise the cream may curdle and the pan may burn slightly, which will ruin the flavour of the soup.

1. Sauté potatoes and onion with bay leaves in butter or margarine for 5 mins

2. Add the sliced leeks to the pan and continue to cook for a further 3-4 mins

3. Pour in vegetable stock, add salt and pepper to taste, then bring to the boil

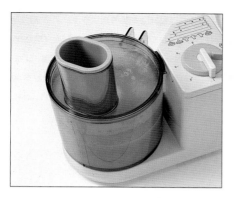

4. Blend two thirds of the cooked vegetables in food processor until smooth

5. After blending vegetables, leave processor on low and gradually add milk

6. Return soup to a clean pan, add the reserved vegetables and heat through

CULLEN SKINK

This Scottish fish and potato soup is hearty enough to be served with crusty bread as a main course. For a smoother version, just whizz the soup through a blender or food processor. It's a treat when there's a nip in the air.

Calories per portion: 266

SERVES 4

1 finnan haddock, approx
   12 oz/350 g
2 small onions
few sprigs of parsley
few black or white peppercorns
¾ pint/450 ml milk
1 lb/450 g potatoes
salt and freshly ground
   black pepper
1 oz/25 g butter
2 tbsp cornflour
freshly chopped parsley

Wash the finnan haddock, then pat dry using absorbent paper. Place on a board and with a very sharp knife, carefully remove the skin. You will find it easier if you hold the tail end firmly with one hand, then place the knife blade at a 45° angle between the skin and flesh. Make short strokes, slicing through between the skin and flesh. As you proceed up the fish, increase the angle of the knife, always remembering to grip the skin firmly. Reserve

the fish skin for making stock.

Peel and slice one of the onions, then place the finnan haddock, onion, parsley sprigs (keep a couple back), and peppercorns in a frying pan. Make up ½ pint/300 ml of the milk to 1 pint/600 ml with water. Pour over the fish then bring to the boil. Reduce heat, then simmer gently for 10-15 mins or until the fish is cooked. Drain, reserving the fish and liquid but discarding the onion, parsley and peppercorns. Reserve any

bones from the fish, flake the flesh into medium-sized pieces, then cover and put to one side.

Meanwhile, place the reserved skin and bones into a pan with remaining onion, parsley sprigs, a few more peppercorns and remaining milk. Add ½ pint/300 ml of water, then bring to the boil and boil gently for 15 mins. Strain into a larger pan.

Peel the potatoes, slice into ¼ in/6 mm pieces then cook in boiling salted water for 10 mins or until tender.

Drain. Add the cooked potatoes, the reserved liquid from cooking the fish, and the flakes of finnan haddock to the fish stock. Bring to a gentle boil, then season to taste. (Be careful with the amount of salt as finnan haddock can be quite salty.) Add the butter, then cook gently until piping hot.

Blend the cornflour to a smooth paste with 4 tbsp of water, stir into the soup and cook until thickened. Serve immediately sprinkled with freshly chopped parsley.

HANDY TIPS

Traditionally, the soup is thickened with potatoes. To do this, cook 1½ lb/675 g potatoes in total, and mash them. Add to the soup with flaked finnan haddock and cook as recipe, omitting cornflour. If finnan haddock is unobtainable, use undyed smoked haddock.

1. Wash and dry the finnan haddock, place on a board and remove skin

2. Place fish in a pan with one onion, parsley, peppercorns, milk and water

3. When fish is cooked, drain, place on a plate. Remove bones, flake fish

4. Place skin and bones in pan with remaining onion, parsley, peppercorns, milk and water

5. Strain the cooked fish stock through a fine sieve into a larger pan. Leave to one side while cooking potatoes

6. Add cooked potato to fish stock, with the reserved cooking liquid and fish. Bring to the boil then season to taste

CHICKEN CHOWDER

When it's cold outside, there's nothing more satisfying than coming home to a bowl of hot home-made soup. Full of succulent pieces of chicken, crisp sweetcorn and chunks of potato, this soup is easy to make and good for you.

Calories per portion: 441

SERVES 6

2½ lb/1.25 kg free-range chicken

3 medium onions

1 carrot

1 stick celery

few sprigs of parsley and thyme

3 bay leaves

2 fresh or frozen corn on the cob

2 oz/50 g butter or margarine

12 oz/350 g potatoes

2 oz/50 g plain white flour

salt and freshly ground
   black pepper

¼ pint/150 ml single cream
   or buttermilk

Remove any giblets from the chicken and discard fat from inside the cavity. Wash chicken under cold running water, then place in a large saucepan. Cover completely with water. Peel the onions, place one in the pan, chop the remaining two and reserve.

Peel the carrot and trim and scrub celery. Cut the celery in half then place the herbs on the inside of one piece, place the other half on top and tie together with string to form a bouquet garni. Add the carrot and bouquet garni to the pan, bring to the boil, cover, then simmer gently for 1 hr or until the chicken is cooked. Allow the chicken to cool for about 20 mins in the pan, then remove and leave until cool enough to handle. Strain and reserve the cooking liquid. When the chicken is cool, strip off and discard the skin. Remove the meat from the bones and cut into small pieces. Cover and reserve in the fridge.

If using fresh corn on the cob, remove husks and silky threads, wash, then cook in boiling water for 15 mins or until tender. Drain, and when cool enough to handle, carefully cut kernels away from the cobs. (If using frozen corn on the cob, cook in boiling water for 5 mins, leave to cool, then cut the kernels away.) Do not add salt to pan.

Melt fat in a large pan, peel then slice the potatoes, add to pan with the reserved chopped onion and cook for 5 mins or until onion is soft. Add the flour and continue cooking for 2 mins. Draw the pan off heat, then gradually stir in 2 pints/1.2 litres reserved cooking liquid, making up with water if necessary. Bring to the boil, stirring throughout, then add the chicken, sweetcorn and seasoning if necessary, and cook for a further 5 mins. Draw pan off heat, stir in the cream or buttermilk, reheat gently then serve.

HANDY TIP

Try adding one red and one green pepper, deseeded and chopped, for more flavour. Add to pan with the chopped chicken meat and seasoning.

1. Place the chicken in a large pan. Add the onion, carrot and bouquet garni

2. Strip off the chicken skin and discard. Remove meat and cut into pieces

3. Cook the corn until tender, drain. Cool, then carefully cut kernels from cob

4. Melt fat, then add the chopped onion and potato. Fry gently for 5 mins

5. Add flour to pan and continue to cook over a gentle heat for 2 mins

6. Add chicken pieces, then stir in sweetcorn kernels, and adjust seasoning

VEGETABLE SOUP

Hot and filling, this recipe for a thick vegetable soup uses the very best of winter produce. Serve it with wholemeal bread for a really satisfying meal. It's guaranteed to keep you warm and glowing on the coldest of days.

Calories per portion: 189

SERVES 6

1 lb/450 g potatoes

8 oz/225 g carrots

8 oz/225 g swede

6 oz/175 g parsnips

1 large onion

3 sticks celery

2 oz/50 g butter or
  polyunsaturated margarine

1¼ pints/750 ml vegetable stock

2 bay leaves

salt and freshly ground
  black pepper

¾ pint/450 ml milk

2 tbsp freshly chopped parsley

HANDY TIPS

To chop an onion without tears, either leave the onion in the fridge for 1 hr before peeling and chopping, or peel the onion, but leave the root on. Make horizontal then vertical cuts towards the root. Then slice right through in the opposite direction.

To remove the smell of onions or even garlic from a chopping board, knife and your hands, straight after chopping rub the board, knife and your hands with dry mustard powder, then add a little cold water to make a paste, rub again, then rinse thoroughly with cold water. And to remove the smell of garlicky breath, just chew some fresh parsley.

Peel the potatoes, carrots, swede, parsnips and onion, then chop. Trim the celery and chop.

Melt the butter or margarine in a large pan then fry the potatoes, onion and celery and cook for 5 mins until slightly softened. Add the remaining vegetables to the pan then continue to fry for a further 5 mins. Pour in the stock, add the bay leaves with salt and black pepper to taste.

Bring to the boil, cover, then reduce heat and simmer gently for 15-20 mins until vegetables are soft. Discard bay leaves. With a draining spoon remove 2 tbsp of the vegetables and reserve.

Place the remaining vegetables and the liquid in a food processor or liquidizer and blend until smooth. If there is too much to purée in one go, purée in two batches. Alternatively, mash the cooked vegetables with a vegetable masher, then pass through a fine sieve into a bowl. If using a processor or liquidizer, after puréeing the vegetables, gradually add the milk and blend for 2 mins until smooth. If not using one, gradually stir the milk into the vegetable soup in the bowl.

When the milk has been added, return the soup to the cleaned pan with the reserved vegetables and chopped parsley. Adjust the seasoning, then reheat gently without allowing the soup to boil. Serve soup hot.

You can use most types of raw vegetables when making this soup, but avoid using too much turnip as this can give a bitter tang.

1. Peel the potatoes, carrots, swede, parsnips and onion. Trim celery then chop

2. Fry the potatoes, onion and celery. Cook for 5 mins until slightly softened

3. Add remaining vegetables to the pan and continue to fry for a further 5 mins

4. Pour in stock, season and bring to the boil, cover, then simmer gently

5. Purée cooked vegetables with the liquid in a food processor until smooth

6. Gradually add the milk to the processor and blend for a further 2 mins

BOUILLABAISSE

Try a taste of true French cuisine with this delicious fish soup flavoured with herbs and spices. Served with chunks of crusty bread, it'll make a hearty and sustaining lunch or supper snack.

Calories per portion: 265　　　　　　　　　**SERVES 6**

few saffron strands

2 lb/900 g mixed fish, cleaned, such as red mullet, monkfish or cod, depending on availability

8 oz/225 g fresh mussels

8 oz/225 g fresh clams

2 large onions, peeled

2 sticks celery

8 oz/225 g tomatoes

2 garlic cloves

2 tbsp olive or vegetable oil

2 bay leaves

1 orange

salt and freshly ground black pepper

few whole prawns

1 tbsp freshly chopped parsley

Place saffron in a small bowl, pour ¼ pint/150 ml boiling water over it and leave to infuse for 30 mins.

Clean fish by removing any scales with a round-bladed knife. Wash well under cold water. If using monkfish remove any skin, discard centre bone and cut into 2 in/5 cm cubes. Leave mullet whole. Skin cod if using, and cut into 2 in/5 cm cubes. Scrub mussels and clams, discarding any that are open, remove beards from mussels and leave in separate bowls of cold water.

Chop the onions, wash and trim celery, then chop finely. With a sharp knife, make a small cross in stalk end of tomatoes. Place in bowl, pour boiling water over them and leave for 2 mins. Remove and discard skins, then chop. Peel and crush garlic.

Heat oil in a large pan, add the onions and celery and gently fry for 5 mins until onions are soft but still transparent. Add bay leaves, garlic and tomatoes, stir lightly.

Using a julienne cutter, add julienne strips of orange rind to pan. Alternatively, finely grate orange rind and add to pan. Add seasoning. Fry for 5 mins.

Arrange the prepared fish, except for shellfish, in a thick layer over the vegetables in the pan. Strain the saffron liquid through a sieve, and then add to the pan with enough water to just cover the fish.

Bring to the boil, cook uncovered for 8 mins. Drain the shellfish, then add to the pan and continue cooking for a further 5-8 mins, or until the fish is cooked but still retains its shape. Add the whole prawns for last 2 mins of the cooking time. Discard any shellfish that have not opened. Sprinkle with chopped parsley and serve in a warmed soup tureen with brown bread.

HANDY TIP

Saffron is a natural colouring and is obtained from the stigmas of yellow crocuses. If saffron is unavailable use ¼-½ tsp turmeric dissolved completely in ¼ pint/150 ml hot water.

1. Remove scales from red mullet with round-bladed knife, starting from tail

2. Scrub mussels and clams, discard open ones. Remove beards from mussels

3. Chop onions and celery. Pour boiling water over tomatoes, discard skins

4. Heat oil in a large pan then fry onion and celery for 5 mins or until softened

5. Add tomatoes, garlic, bay leaves, orange rind, seasoning. Fry for 5 mins

6. Arrange fish in thick layer over vegetables. Strain saffron liquid, add to pan

CREAM OF CUCUMBER SOUP

This delicious, creamy soup with its light, delicate flavour highlights the very best of summer. Quick and easy to prepare, it's perfect served with Melba toast.

Calories per portion: 265

SERVES 6

1. Cut bread from the stale loaf into very thin slices, remove crusts and place on a baking sheet

2. To flavour the milk, infuse with one peeled onion and 2 fresh bay leaves. Bring to just below boiling point

3. Peel the cucumber, cut in half lengthways then scoop out the seeds and discard. Chop cucumber flesh

1 stale white loaf, uncut

1 pint/600 ml milk

2 onions

2 fresh bay leaves

1 large or 1½ medium-sized
   cucumbers

2 sticks celery

3 oz/75 g butter or margarine

1 lemon

1 pint/600 ml vegetable stock

2 oz/50 g plain flour

salt and freshly ground
   black pepper

1 tsp freshly grated nutmeg

¼ pint/150 ml single cream

a few sprigs tarragon

Set oven to Gas 1, 275°F, 140°C. Use the bread to make Melba toast: place loaf on bread-board and cut the thinnest slices you can. Remove crusts, then place slices on a baking sheet in the bottom of the oven for 1½ hrs to dry out.

Pour the milk into a small pan. Peel one of the onions and add to pan. Wash and dry bay leaves and add to pan. Bring milk to just below boiling point, remove from the heat. Cover and leave to infuse for 15 mins.

Peel the cucumbers very thinly, cut in half lengthways, then scoop out and discard seeds, using a teaspoon. Chop flesh.

Wash and trim celery and chop. Peel, then chop remaining onion.

Melt 1 oz/25 g of the butter or margarine in a large pan, then fry the chopped vegetables for 5 mins. Wash and dry the lemon, then grate the rind finely into the pan. Squeeze the lemon. Pour in the stock and lemon juice, bring to the boil, cover and simmer gently for 10-15 mins or until soft.

Meanwhile, melt the remaining butter or margarine in a small pan. Stir in the flour and cook, stirring, for 2 mins. Remove from the heat. Strain the infused milk, then gradually mix into the roux, beating well between each addition. Return pan to the heat and cook, stirring throughout, until the sauce is thick, smooth and glossy. Season with salt, pepper and the freshly grated nutmeg.

Pour the cooked cucumber and stock into a food processor. Add the sauce, then purée until smooth. If the soup is to be served hot, reheat gently, add cream and allow to come

to just below boiling point.

If soup is to be served cold, cool quickly after puréeing by transferring to a clean bowl and standing bowl in a sink with enough cold water to come halfway up the sides of the bowl until cool. Stir in the cream, chill in the fridge, covered, for at least 2 hrs. Garnish with sprigs of tarragon and a few slices of cucumber. Serve with Melba toast.

HANDY TIP

When making Melba toast it is essential that you use bread that is 1-2 days old so that you can slice the loaf really thinly. The toast can be made with brown bread if preferred.

4. Melt the fat then after sweating the vegetables for 5 mins, grate the lemon rind finely into the pan

5. Pour in the vegetable stock and the lemon juice, bring to the boil, cover and simmer for 10-15 mins, or until soft

6. Place cooked cucumber and stock in to a food processor, add the sauce, purée until smooth, add cream

PEA AND HAM SOUP

Warm them up in winter with our delicious, nourishing soup. It's so full of flavour and will keep the healthiest appetite happy. Serve hot for lunch or supper with crusty chunks of freshly baked brown bread. The whole family will love it.

Calories per portion: 446   **SERVES 4**

6 oz/175 g dried green lentils
few sprigs parsley
few sprigs rosemary
2 bay leaves
8 oz/225 g piece unsmoked
  bacon, such as collar
1 large onion
1 garlic clove
2 large carrots
8 oz/225 g leeks
2 oz/50 g butter or margarine
3 pints/1.7 litres vegetable stock
salt and freshly ground
  black pepper

Pick the lentils over discarding any stones or grit. Wash thoroughly under cold running water. Place in a large bowl then cover with water. Leave lentils to soak, preferably overnight. Drain and put to one side.

Place the herbs in a small square of muslin. Tie up to form a bouquet garni.

Trim bacon, discarding any fat, rind or gristle. Cut into small cubes, approx ½ in/1.25 cm. Peel and chop the onion. Peel and crush garlic. Peel carrots, trim, then cut into small dice. Trim leeks, wash well under cold running water. Slice thinly.

Heat fat in a large pan, add the bacon and vegetables. Fry gently, stirring occasionally for 5-8 mins or until vegetables have softened but are still transparent. Add the drained soaked lentils and mix well together. Place the prepared bouquet garni in the pan then pour in the stock. Bring to the boil, cover, then reduce heat and simmer

gently for 1–1½ hrs or until lentils are soft and mushy and the soup is a thick consistency. Discard bouquet garni and add salt and pepper to taste. Serve piping hot with fresh brown bread.

1. Wash the lentils thoroughly then cover with water and leave to soak

2. Make a bouquet garni with the parsley and rosemary sprigs and bay leaves

3. Trim the bacon, discarding any fat, rind or gristle. Cut into small cubes

4. Fry the onion, garlic, carrot, leeks and bacon gently in the fat until softened

5. Add the soaked and drained lentils to the softened vegetables and mix well

6. Place the bouquet garni in the pan, add the stock and bring to the boil

GAZPACHO

Sun-ripened tomatoes, crisp tangy peppers, cool fresh cucumber and a hint of garlic. These are the ingredients for a perfect Gazpacho. Serve it iced with plenty of croûtons. It's ideal as a starter for hot sunny days.

Calories per portion: 306　　　　　　　　　　　　　　　**SERVES 4**

1 ½ lb/675 g ripe tomatoes

1 large Spanish onion

1 large garlic clove, peeled and crushed

½ cucumber, peeled

1 green pepper, deseeded

juice 1 lemon, strained

2-3 tbsp white wine vinegar

3-4 tbsp olive oil

½ pint/300 ml tomato juice

salt and freshly ground black pepper

½ red pepper, deseeded

3 slices white or brown bread

2 tbsp vegetable oil

ice cubes

Make a small cross on the top of each tomato. Place in a large bowl and pour over boiling water. Leave to stand for 2 minutes. Using a draining spoon, remove the tomatoes from the bowl, peel away the skins and discard. Cut the tomatoes into quarters, discard the seeds and cores.

Peel and chop the onion and place in food processor or liquidizer with the tomato quarters and garlic. Blend for 2-3 mins to make a purée.

Cut the cucumber in half lengthways and discard the seeds. Dice or chop finely and add 2 tbsp to the tomato purée. Reserve remainder for serving. Dice or finely chop the green pepper, add 2 tbsp to the tomato purée, reserving the remainder.

Add the lemon juice, vinegar, olive oil, tomato juice with salt and freshly ground black pepper to taste. Blend for 2-3 mins or until a smooth purée forms. Check seasoning, pour into soup tureen and chill for at least 2 hours.

Finely chop the red pepper and mix with the reserved green pepper.

Discard the crusts and cut the bread into ¼ in/6 mm cubes. Heat the vegetable oil in a frying pan. Fry bread cubes for 5-8 mins, stirring throughout until golden brown and crisp. Drain well on absorbent paper.

Just before serving add ice cubes to the Gazpacho and sprinkle the top with a little cucumber, pepper and croûtons. Serve remaining cucumber, peppers and croûtons separately with some hot crusty French bread.

HANDY TIP

Gazpacho can be made in advance and kept in the fridge. Stir before serving, add ice cubes, and garnish.

1. If tomato skin doesn't peel easily, return to hot water for another minute

2. Discard tomato core, and reserve seeds to flavour stews or casseroles

3. Chop onion finely – leaving the root on while doing so helps prevent tears

4. *Cucumber skin and seeds can be bitter, so discard them and dice flesh*

5. *Blend the Gazpacho on a high speed to ensure that a smooth purée forms*

6. *Fry bread cubes quickly and drain well for really crisp, golden croûtons*

TARAMASALATA

Smoked cod's roe, garlic, bread-crumbs and olive oil, flavoured with lemon, make this popular dish. Traditionally served in Greece as an appetizer with pitta bread.

Calories per portion: 526   **SERVES 6**

FOR THE MELBA TOAST:
**½ uncut large white loaf,
    preferably at least 2 days old**
FOR THE TARAMASALATA:
**12 oz/350 g smoked cod's roe
1 medium onion
3 oz/75 g fresh white
    breadcrumbs
2 garlic cloves
1 large lemon
8 fl oz/250 ml olive oil
rock salt
freshly ground black pepper
lemon slices and parsley
    to decorate**

Preheat oven to Gas 1, 275°F, 140°C. To make Melba toast, place the loaf on a bread-board, cut the thinnest slices you can. Trim and discard the crusts then place slices on a baking sheet on the bottom shelf of the oven and leave for 2 hrs to dry out. Check the bread occasionally to ensure it doesn't burn.

If you prefer, the bread can be dried out any time you are using your oven at a low temperature. Once cold, store in an airtight tin until required. It will keep in the tin for 2-3 weeks.

To make the Taramasalata, skin the cod's roe and break up into small

pieces. Place in the bowl of a food processor and process for a few minutes until smooth.

Peel and finely chop the onion, add to the cod's roe together with breadcrumbs. Peel and crush the garlic cloves, add to the mixture then process again until smooth.

Finely grate the rind from the lemon and squeeze then strain the juice, add to the processor and process again until smooth. (It is important to only switch the processor on for short bursts, and to ensure that no mixture is caught underneath the blade, as the mixture at this stage is fairly stiff. If you just leave the processor running it could be too much for the motor.)

Gradually add the olive oil, drop by drop, to the mixture, scraping down the sides of the bowl if necessary. When all the oil has been added, gradually blend in approx 6 tbsp tepid boiled water to form a smooth dropping consistency. Add a little freshly milled rock salt and ground black pepper, check for taste. Turn into a serving bowl, cover and chill for at least 1 hr before serving. Decorate with lemon slices and parsley and serve with Melba toast.

1. Cut very thin slices from the bread then trim and discard the crusts, place on the baking sheet

2. Skin the cod's roe, break up into small pieces, place in food processor, and process until smooth

3. Peel and finely chop the onion, then add to the cod's roe together with the breadcrumbs and garlic

---

HANDY TIP

You can also make Taramasalata by hand. Beat the cod's roe until smooth, then add the oil drop by drop. Add remaining ingredients when you've added half of the oil.

4. Finely grate the lemon rind, add to the mixture together with the strained lemon juice

5. Add the olive oil, drop by drop, blending throughout until a smooth dropping consistency is achieved

6. Add freshly milled rock salt and ground black pepper to the Taramasalata then chill before serving

Coquilles Saint-Jacques

Slices of scallops poached gently in white wine with succulent sliced button mushrooms and coated in a delicate white sauce make this spectacular dish.

Calories per portion: 255   SERVES 4

4 prepared scallops in shells
¼ pint/150 ml dry white wine
1 onion, peeled and sliced
1 carrot, peeled and sliced
few parsley stalks
sprig of thyme
4 oz/100 g button mushrooms
1½ oz/40 g butter
1 oz/25 g plain flour
1 egg yolk, size 3
salt and freshly ground
   black pepper
extra 1 oz/25 g butter, optional
2 tbsp fresh breadcrumbs
2 tbsp melted butter
lemon and cucumber twists
   to garnish

Preheat oven to Gas 9, 475°F, 240°C, 15 mins before serving. Using a small sharp knife, remove the scallops from their shells then wash lightly and dry on absorbent paper. Clean and trim the scallops, if liked the skirt can be used in the stock.

Place the dry white wine with ¼ pint/150 ml of water in a frying pan with the peeled and sliced onion and carrot, parsley and thyme. Bring to the boil, simmer gently for 8 mins. Add the washed scallops and simmer for 4 mins. Remove the scallops, strain and reserve the cooking liquid. Cut the corals away from the scallop white meat and reserve. Cut the white meat into slices.

Wipe the mushrooms and slice thinly. Heat the butter then gently cook the mushrooms for 2 mins, drain, place in a small bowl. Add the sliced scallops and toss in the melted butter. Drain and reserve. Add the flour to the remaining fat in pan and cook for 2 mins. Remove from heat then gradually stir in the reserved cooking liquid. Return the pan to the heat and cook stirring throughout until the sauce thickens. Remove from the heat, cool slightly then beat in the egg yolk. Return to the heat and cook for a further 2 mins to cook the egg. Take

care not to boil the sauce otherwise you may have small pieces of cooked egg in the sauce rather than a smooth sauce. Season to taste and if using, whisk in the further 1 oz/25 g butter.

If using scallop shells for serving, scrub well, plunge into boiling water for 2 mins, drain and dry well.

Place a little sauce in the base of each shell, top with the mushrooms, then the white meat and lastly the coral. Cover completely with the remaining sauce. Sprinkle the top with the breadcrumbs and pour a little melted butter over each. Cook in oven for 6-8 mins or until piping hot and golden brown on top. Serve garnished with cucumber and lemon twists.

HANDY TIP

When buying the scallops, ask the fishmonger for the concave scallop shells so you can use them as serving dishes.

1. Using a small sharp knife, remove the scallops from their shells, wash lightly and dry on absorbent paper

2. Clean and trim the scallops, if liked use the skirt in the stock. Place white wine, water and vegetables in pan

3. Gently poach the scallops in the white wine and water with the onion, carrot and herbs, simmer for 8 mins

4. Cut the corals away from the scallop white meat and reserve. Cut the white meat into slices

5. Scrub shells, plunge into boiling water, dry. Place a spoonful of prepared sauce in the base of each cleaned scallop shell

6. Arrange the sliced mushrooms, then the sliced white meat, then the coral, coat with sauce

SMOKED FISH PATE

Deliciously light flakes of smoked haddock and mackerel, with a subtle tang of lime, make this pâté a luscious starter for any meal. Served with crispy Melba toast, it's sure to impress everyone.

Calories per portion: 685 — SERVES 4

1 lb/450 g piece of undyed
   smoked haddock
½ pint/300 ml semi-skimmed
   milk
1 bay leaf
1 sprig each of dill, parsley
   and thyme
½ medium onion, peeled and
   studded with 4 cloves
12 oz/350 g smoked
   mackerel fillets
zested rind and juice
   of 1 lime
4 oz/100 g butter or
   margarine, softened
4 oz/100 g fromage frais
4 tbsp mixed peppercorns
FOR THE CUPS:
6 slices white bread
cherry tomatoes and parsley
   to garnish

Wash and dry the haddock then place in a frying pan with the milk, herbs and onion. Bring to the boil, then reduce heat and simmer gently for 10-15 mins or until cooked. Allow to cool in the cooking liquid, before draining and discarding liquid. Discard skin and any bones from the haddock, flake finely.

Discard the skin from the smoked mackerel and carefully scrape away any of the dark flesh on the skinned side. Flake mackerel and then mix with the haddock. Sprinkle with the lime rind and juice, cover lightly and leave for 30 mins for the flavours to develop.

Cream 2 oz/50 g of the fat until soft, stir in the fish and fromage frais. Mix well, spoon into four individual pâté or ramekin dishes. Smooth the tops, cover, chill in the fridge for 30 mins.

Melt remaining fat, pour over the

HANDY TIP

If liked substitute the smoked haddock with cod and replace the mackerel with smoked trout.

pâté to completely cover tops. Lightly crush the peppercorns in a pestle and mortar, sprinkle on top of the fat. Chill the pâtés for a further 30 mins.

Meanwhile, make the Melba cups by toasting the bread on both sides until golden. Using a 4 in/10 cm round plain pastry cutter, cut out a circle from each slice. Holding toasted rounds flat, slide a knife between the toasted edges to split the bread. Return to the grill and toast untoasted side uppermost, until golden, and the edges have curled up. Serve warm with the pâté, garnished with cherry tomatoes and parsley.

1. Simmer the haddock in the milk with the onion and herbs for 10-15 mins

2. Drain fish then carefully remove skin from the haddock and discard. Flake fish

3. Skin mackerel and flake, mix with haddock, sprinkle with lime rind and juice

4. Spoon the prepared pâté into four individual dishes, pressing the mixture down with the back of a spoon

5. Cover pâtés with melted butter then lightly crush peppercorns and sprinkle over the top

6. Make Melba cups by splitting toasted rounds of bread then toasting again until edges curl

CHICKEN SATAY

Super, spicy Chicken Satay is a delicious Far Eastern dish served with a delicate nutty sauce. You can cook it over charcoal or under the grill to make an impressive and unusual supper or first course. Your friends and family will love it.

Calories per portion: 384　　　　　　　　**SERVES 4**

1 shallot
1 in/2.5 cm piece root ginger
1-2 garlic cloves
1-2 fresh chillis
1 tsp chilli powder, optional
1½ tsp turmeric
2 tsp light soft brown sugar
2 tbsp white malt vinegar
1 tbsp lemon juice
2 tbsp vegetable oil
½ pint/300 ml coconut milk or
　semi-skimmed milk
4 oz/100 g roasted peanuts
1 lb/450 g chicken
　breasts, skinned
fresh chilli rings to garnish

Peel then roughly chop the shallot and the root ginger. Peel the garlic (the amount you use depends on how garlicky you like your food) and roughly chop. Deseed and chop the fresh chillis. Place the chopped ingredients in a mortar.

Add chilli powder, if using, and turmeric, then pound with pestle until thoroughly blended. (Alternatively, place spices in a food processor and blend together.)

HANDY TIP

If liked, thin strips of lean lamb, cut from the leg or shoulder, or beef (use rump steak), can be used instead of the chicken. The lamb will take 16-20 mins to cook. All types of satay can also be barbecued over charcoal.

Add sugar, then mix in vinegar, lemon juice, oil and milk.

Place the roasted peanuts in a food processor or coffee grinder and grind to a coarse or fine consistency, depending on whether you prefer a smooth or chunky sauce. Stir the peanuts into the marinade and mix thoroughly.

Place the prepared marinade in a saucepan, bring to the boil, then simmer very gently for 8-10 mins, stirring occasionally. Remove from heat and allow to cool.

Trim off and discard any fat from chicken, wash flesh and pat dry with kitchen paper. Using a sharp knife, cut into long, thin strips. Place chicken in a shallow dish and spoon half the cooled peanut marinade over. Cover, then chill in the fridge for at least 2 hrs, turning occasionally. Cover and chill the remaining marinade.

Cover 8 wooden kebab sticks with cold water and soak for 2 hrs (to prevent the kebab sticks from catching alight during cooking).

When ready to cook the satay, preheat grill to medium. Drain the chicken, reserving marinade, and thread on to the soaked kebab sticks. Place on grill pan and grill for 10-12 mins, or until cooked, turning frequently and brushing occasionally with marinade.

Place remaining marinade in a small pan, bring to the boil and cook for about 2 mins. Pour into a small bowl, garnish with fresh chilli rings and serve with the Chicken Satay.

1. Pound the chopped shallot, ginger, garlic, chillis and spices in a mortar

2. Place the peanuts in a food processor and process to required consistency

3. Trim fat from chicken breasts. Using a sharp knife, cut into long, thin strips

4. Place chicken in dish, spoon half the marinade over. Cover, then chill

5. Thread chicken on to soaked wooden kebab sticks. Reserve marinade

6. Place kebabs on grill pan and cook under preheated grill, turning frequently

PLAICE GOUJONS

Thin strips of fish encased in egg and breadcrumbs, then fried until crisp and golden... this recipe is ideal when time is short. Add chips, a twist of lemon and a bowl of tartare sauce, and you'll serve up a mouthwatering treat.

Calories per portion: 537

SERVES 4

FOR THE TARTARE SAUCE:

I egg yolk, size 3

½ level tsp dried mustard

½ level tsp salt

freshly ground black pepper

½ level tsp caster sugar

1-1½ tbsp white wine vinegar or lemon juice

¼ pint/150 ml olive oil

2 tbsp freshly chopped tarragon

I tbsp freshly chopped parsley

1-2 gherkins, finely chopped

a few capers, finely chopped

FOR THE GOUJONS:

I lb/450 g plaice fillets

I oz/25 g flour

I egg, size 3

4 oz/100 g breadcrumbs

oil for deep frying

tarragon sprig and twist of lemon to garnish

Place egg yolk in a bowl with the mustard, salt, pepper and sugar. Add I tsp vinegar or lemon juice, mix well. Gradually add oil, one drop at a time to begin with. Whisk constantly until smooth and thick. After adding half the oil, the remainder can be added in a thin steady stream, but whisk continuously while oil is being added.

If the mayonnaise becomes too thick, add a little more vinegar or lemon juice. Once all the oil has been used, stir in the remaining vinegar or lemon juice with the chopped herbs, gherkins and capers. Cover and leave to stand for I hr to allow flavours to blend and develop.

To make the goujons, place fish fillets on a board then, holding the skin at the tail end, remove skin with a sharp knife. Cut the fillets into 3 in x ½ in/7.5 cm x 1.25 cm strips. If

HANDY TIP

If liked, cod or haddock can be used instead of plaice. Cook for 4-6 mins. Or try using thin strips of skinned and boned chicken breast. Cook for 4-6 mins.

necessary, trim the edges to give a neat shape. Place flour in a small bowl and season. Beat egg and place in a shallow bowl, place breadcrumbs in another bowl. Coat strips of plaice in seasoned flour, then dip in beaten egg and coat in breadcrumbs. If liked, coat again.

Heat oil in a deep fat fryer to 350°F, 180°C. Fry the fish in small batches for 3-5 minutes or until crisp and golden. Drain well on absorbent paper. Repeat until all the strips have been cooked. Garnish and serve with the tartare sauce and freshly fried chips.

1. Mix the egg yolk with mustard, seasoning, sugar and vinegar. Whisk in oil

2. When oil has been incorporated, stir in remaining vinegar, herbs and pickles

3. Place fillets on a board. Hold firmly with one hand, then skin with a sharp knife

4. Cut the fillets into 3 in x ½ in/7.5 cm x 1.25 cm strips and trim edges to neaten

5. Dip strips into seasoned flour, then beaten egg and finally in breadcrumbs

6. Heat oil to 350°F, 180°C. Fry goujons for 3-5 minutes or until crisp and golden

SWEET & SOUR PRAWNS

Tender succulent prawns, with a hint of ginger and garlic, coated in a light, crisp golden batter and served with a delicious tangy sweet and sour sauce and fried rice. This dish is quick and easy to cook.

Calories per portion: 379   **SERVES 6**

2 tbsp light soy sauce
3 tbsp dry sherry
2 tbsp groundnut oil
1 in/2.5 cm piece root ginger
1-2 garlic cloves
3-4 spring onions
1 lb/450 g peeled prawns, thawed
    if frozen
FOR THE SAUCE:
½ small red pepper
½ small green pepper
1 carrot
¼ pint/150 ml fish stock
1 tbsp light soy sauce
2 tbsp white wine vinegar
1 tbsp clear honey
1 tbsp tomato purée
1-2 tsp cornflour
FOR THE BATTER:
5 tbsp cornflour
2 eggs, size 5, beaten
oil for deep fat frying

HANDY TIP

As a tasty alternative to the prawns, why not use small cubes of raw cod, or boned monkfish.

Mix the soy sauce, sherry and oil together in a medium-sized glass bowl. Peel and finely grate the root ginger, peel and crush the garlic. Trim the spring onions, wash well, dry, then chop finely. Add the ginger, garlic and spring onions to the bowl and mix well.

Dry the prawns thoroughly, add to the bowl and stir well. Cover and chill for at least 1 hr, turning occasionally.

To make the sauce, cut tops off the peppers, discard seeds and pith, then cut into thin strips. Peel carrot, slice thinly, cut into thin strips. Place in a small bowl, pour boiling water over, leave for 5 mins, then drain.

Mix the stock, soy sauce, vinegar, honey and tomato purée together in a small saucepan, bring to the boil, then simmer for 5 mins.

Mix the cornflour to a paste with 2 tsp of water, stir into the pan and cook until thickened. Add the drained pepper and carrot strips, stir well then leave on one side.

To make the batter, sift the cornflour into a mixing bowl, add the eggs and beat well until smooth.

Drain prawns then place small amounts in the batter and coat well. Heat the oil in a deep fat fryer to 350°F, 180°C. Drop small spoonfuls of the coated prawns into the batter and fry for 4-5 mins until golden brown. Drain on absorbent paper, and repeat with remaining prawns. Warm the sauce through, then pour a little over the cooked prawns. Serve remaining sauce with rice, to accompany prawns.

1. Mix the soy sauce, sherry and oil together. Add the ginger, garlic and onion

2. Drain prawns, place in marinade and leave, covered, for at least 1 hr

3. Deseed peppers, remove pith then cut into strips. Peel carrot and cut into strips

4. Mix the cornflour and eggs together to form a smooth batter. Beat well

5. After marinating, drain prawns, then place in prepared batter and coat well

6. Heat oil and fry the prawns for 4-5 mins or until golden brown. Drain well

FRIED CALAMARI

Follow this easy step-by-step guide and give your family a delicious taste of one of the most popular of all Mediterranean dishes. Served with slices of lemon as a starter or crusty bread and a salad for a main meal, it's a real fish favourite.

Calories per portion: 480

SERVES 4

2 lb/900 g squid
FOR THE BATTER:
4 oz/100 g plain flour
1 tsp baking powder
pinch of salt
1 egg, size 3
1 tbsp olive oil
oil for deep frying
TO GARNISH:
parsley sprigs
lemon slices

First prepare the squid by pulling the head and tentacles (arms) away from the body. Peel off and discard the thin mottled skin. Rinse the squid in cold water, draw back the rim of the body pouch and locate the top end of the quill-shaped pen. Grasp gently then pull the pen and any entrails free from the surrounding flesh, discard. Wash again. If tentacles are reasonably large, use these. Place the squid's head and viscera (which contains the ink sac) on a chopping board and cut tentacles away from just below the eye. Discard the head and viscera (a bony beak-like mouth, complete with teeth, that lies within the flesh connecting the base of the tentacles). Slice the tentacles and the body into rings. Wash and dry on kitchen paper.

To make the batter, sift the flour, baking powder and salt into a bowl. Make a well in the centre and add egg. Mix the oil with ¼ pint/150 ml water and add to the egg. Beat well, gradually incorporating the flour to make a smooth batter.

Heat oil in a deep fat fryer to 350°F, 180°C. (If you don't have a thermometer, the oil is ready when a small spoonful of the batter dropped into the oil sizzles and rises to the surface in 30 seconds.) Coat a few of the squid rings in batter (use a slotted spoon or your fingers, whichever you prefer), then place in the oil.

HANDY TIPS

The flesh of squid should be firm to the touch. Only the tentacles and fleshy body sac are eaten. The tentacles are usually chopped, then cooked. The body section can be sliced or stuffed – try a lemon and coriander stuffing.

In some Mediterranean recipes the ink is used – remove intact before cooking. If the squid has been previously frozen, the ink will have coagulated. To thaw, place the frozen granules of ink in a little hot water until liquid.

Cook rings in oil for 1-2 mins or until puffed up and golden. Drain on kitchen paper and keep warm while cooking remaining rings.

Serve the calamari hot, garnished with parsley sprigs and lemon slices.

1. Pull head and tentacles away from body. Carefully peel off skin, discard

2. Gently pull out the transparent quill and any remaining entrails

3. Place the head and viscera on board, cut tentacles away below eye

4. Discard head and viscera. Slice the tentacles and body into rings

5. Coat the squid rings, a few at a time, in the prepared batter

6. Cook rings in oil for 1-2 mins until puffed up and golden. Drain

SALAD NICOISE

This salad originates from the Côte d'Azur and can be served as a starter or main meal. You can vary the ingredients slightly, but always use flaked tuna, French beans and black olives. It's a tasty change to traditional salads.

Calories per portion: 398 | **SERVES 6**

8 oz/225 g new potatoes

8 oz/225 g French beans

2 garlic cloves

few sprigs of parsley

4-6 slices white bread

2 tbsp olive oil

1 oz/25 g butter or margarine

14 oz/400 g can tuna
  in brine

4 eggs, size 3

1 red pepper

8 oz/225 g firm ripe tomatoes

red and green oak-leaf lettuce

2 oz/50 g can anchovy fillets

few black olives, pitted

FOR THE DRESSING:

1-2 tsp caster sugar

1 tsp dry mustard powder

salt and freshly ground
  black pepper

1-2 garlic cloves

3 tbsp white wine vinegar

6 tbsp olive oil

Wash and scrub the potatoes. Cook in plenty of boiling salted water for 12-15 mins until cooked. Drain and leave to cool completely.

Wash French beans, trim off tops and tails, then cook in boiling salted water for 5-8 mins, or until cooked but still crunchy. Drain and leave until cold.

Peel garlic cloves, crush in a pestle and mortar or garlic press. Finely chop the parsley. Trim crusts from bread then cut into small cubes.

Heat oil and fat in frying pan and fry garlic gently for 2 mins. Add the bread cubes and parsley and continue to fry, turning the bread frequently, until golden brown. Drain on kitchen paper.

Drain tuna and flake into large chunks. Cook eggs in boiling water for 10 mins, plunge into cold water and leave until cold. Shell and quarter.

Deseed pepper, then wash thoroughly and cut into chunks. Wash and dry tomatoes, cut into quarters. Wash lettuce and dry with kitchen paper. Drain anchovy fillets, separate and roll into curls.

Place the lettuce leaves on a large serving platter, arrange all the prepared ingredients, except croûtons, attractively on top. Scatter the olives over.

To make the dressing, place the sugar, mustard, salt and pepper in a screw-top jar. Peel and crush the garlic, then add to jar with the vinegar and oil. Screw the lid on and shake vigorously.

Drizzle a little dressing over the prepared salad and serve the remainder separately. Serve the salad with the garlic croûtons and fresh crusty bread.

HANDY TIP

Make extra dressing then keep the remainder in a screw-top jar for up to 3 weeks in the fridge.

1. Wash French beans, trim tops and tails and cook in boiling salted water

2. Peel and crush garlic, finely chop the parsley and cut bread into cubes

3. Heat fat in frying pan, fry garlic for 2 mins, add bread cubes and parsley

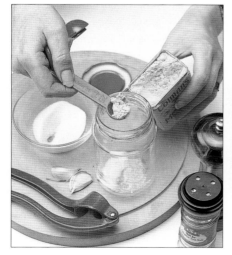

4. Make vinaigrette dressing in a screw-top jar, shake vigorously before use

5. Drain the tuna well, place on a plate, and gently flake into large chunks

6. Boil eggs, then plunge into cold water. Leave until cold, shell and quarter

FISH MOUSSE

Encased in thin slices of smoked salmon, this delicious fish mousse is delicately flavoured with chives and served with a smooth nutty avocado sauce. It's the perfect start to a special dinner party or ideal for a light summer's lunch.

Calories per portion: 305   **SERVES 4**

6 oz/175 g white fish fillet, such as haddock or cod, skinned

¼ pint/150 ml milk, or milk and water mixed together

1 stick celery, trimmed

2 slices onion

1 small carrot, peeled

1 bouquet garni

6 oz/175 g smoked salmon, sliced very thinly

2 tbsp freshly snipped chives

¼ pint/150 ml fromage frais or low-fat natural yogurt, or single cream

2 tsp gelatine

salt and freshly ground black pepper

1 egg white, size 3

dill sprigs and lemon twists to garnish

FOR THE SAUCE:

1 small ripe avocado

1 tbsp lemon juice, strained

3 fl oz/85 ml fromage frais or single cream

HANDY TIP

In very hot weather use a little extra gelatine to ensure a good set.

Place the fish fillet in a frying pan with milk, or milk and water, celery, onion, carrot and bouquet garni. Simmer over a gentle heat for about 10 mins or until cooked. Drain, reserving fish. When cold, discard any bones and flake fish.

Meanwhile, line four ramekin dishes with slices of smoked salmon, reserving a little for the tops. Ensure the slices overlap slightly and that they come over the top a little. Cover and leave to one side.

Place the cold flaked fish in a food processor and blend until smooth. Place in a bowl and add the chives. Stir in fromage frais, yogurt or cream.

Dissolve gelatine in 1½ tbsp hot water, allow to cool slightly then stir into the mixture with salt and black pepper. Whisk egg white until stiff, fold into the mixture.

Spoon into prepared ramekins, fold salmon edges over then place reserved salmon on top to completely encase mousse. Leave in the fridge to set for at least 2 hrs.

To make the sauce, carefully peel the avocado and discard the stone. Place in a food processor with the strained lemon juice and blend until smooth. Add the fromage frais or single cream and then thoroughly blend again.

To serve, turn the fish mousses out on to individual plates. Spoon a little avocado sauce over and garnish with dill sprigs and lemon twists. Serve the remaining sauce separately. Serve the mousses with thin slices of brown bread and butter.

1. Line four individual ramekin dishes with thin slices of smoked salmon

2. Place the flaked cooked fish in a food processor and blend until smooth

3. Place the fish in a mixing bowl then add snipped and washed chives

4. Stir in the fromage frais, yogurt or cream, followed by dissolved gelatine

5. Spoon the mousse mixture into the 4 dishes lined with smoked salmon

6. Fold the edges of the salmon over, and place reserved slice on top

LAMB KEBABS

Serve up a taste of the Mediterranean with our delicious kebabs. Made from tender ground lamb, freshly chopped mint and coriander, with just a hint of lemon, they're simple to prepare and an ideal dish for a mid-week family treat.

Calories per portion: 358   **SERVES 4**

1 lb/450 g ground lean lamb
3 large spring onions
2 sprigs fresh coriander
2 sprigs fresh mint
4 oz/100 g fresh white or
    brown breadcrumbs
1 lemon, preferably unwaxed
salt and freshly ground
    black pepper
1 egg, size 3, beaten
1 tbsp sunflower oil
lemon wedges and radish roses
    to garnish

HANDY TIPS

You can vary the flavour of the kebabs – try adding 2 peeled and crushed garlic cloves to the basic mixture. Replace the herbs with 1½ tsp ground coriander and 1½ tsp ground cumin, or 2 deseeded and chopped chillis and 1 tbsp chopped parsley.
You can also cook the minced lamb kebabs on a barbecue. Make as above. Once the coals have turned grey and are ready to be used, brush the kebabs lightly with oil, then cook over coals for 8-12 mins, turning as necessary.

Preheat the grill to a moderate heat 5-10 mins before cooking the kebabs.

Place the ground lamb in a large mixing bowl. Trim the root and most of the dark green top from the spring onions. Make a slit down one side and discard the outer layer of onion. Wash and dry well, then, using a pair of kitchen scissors, snip into very small pieces and add to the bowl.

Wash and dry the coriander and mint, chop finely, then add to the mixture together with the breadcrumbs. Finely grate the rind from the lemon into the bowl (use a dry pastry brush to remove the rind from the side of the grater). Stir the mixture well, then season to taste with salt and ground black pepper.

Add the egg, then mix together until all the ingredients are well distributed throughout and come together to form a ball in the centre of the bowl. Mould the mixture into small oval shapes, approx 2 in/5 cm in length (you may find it easier and less messy if you wet your hands before shaping the kebabs).

Thread the lamb on to four kebab skewers, taking care not to break up the meat, cover lightly, then chill for at least 1 hr.

Just before cooking, brush the lamb with the oil, then grill, turning frequently, for 10-15 mins, or until golden brown.

Garnish with lemon wedges and radish roses and serve on a bed of freshly cooked pasta, with a salad and warm strips of pitta bread.

1. Trim the spring onions, discard outer layer. Wash and chop the fresh herbs

2. Add onion, herbs and breadcrumbs to lamb. Grate lemon rind into bowl

3. Season, add beaten egg, then stir until mixture comes together to form a ball

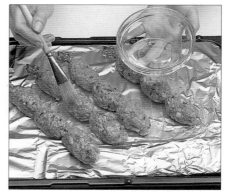

4. Mould the mixture into oval shapes (wet hands slightly for easier moulding)

5. Thread lamb shapes on to kebab sticks, taking care not to break up meat

6. After chilling, place kebabs on rack lined with foil, brush with oil, then grill

MOULES A LA MARINIERE

Mussels really are delicious! They're so simple to prepare and quick to cook. And served with a creamy wine sauce, crusty bread and a glass of white wine, they make a starter that will impress friends and family.

Calories per portion: 570　　　　　　　　　　　　　　　**SERVES 4**

4 lb/1.75 kg fresh mussels
1 tbsp salt
3 oz/75 g unsalted butter
3 shallots, peeled and chopped
1-2 garlic cloves, peeled
　and crushed
½ pint/300 ml dry white wine and
　¼ pint/150 ml fish stock
½ oz/15 g freshly chopped parsley
2 sprigs fresh thyme
2 bay leaves
6 black peppercorns
1 oz/25 g plain flour
¼ pint/150 ml single cream
French bread to serve

Scrub mussels in plenty of cold water, scraping off any barnacles on the shells and removing dirt. Scrape beards off shells with a sharp knife. Discard any mussels that are open at this stage. Dissolve salt in water in a large bowl or sink, then leave mussels to soak for at least 30 mins to remove any sand or grit. (This stage is extremely important. If you don't soak the mussels, they will be gritty when you eat them.) Drain the mussels, discarding any that have now opened.

Melt 2 oz/50 g of the butter in a 4 pint/2.25 litre saucepan. Sauté the shallots and garlic for 3-5 mins, until soft and transparent but not browned. Add the wine and stock, half the parsley, the thyme, bay leaves and peppercorns. Cover and simmer for 10 mins. Strain, then add drained mussels a handful at a time to the liquid; bring to the boil. Cover with a close-fitting lid, cook over a constant heat for 3-5 mins, shaking the pan occasionally or until the mussels have opened. Now discard any which remain shut. Drain, reserving liquid.

Discard top half of shells, place mussels in tureen or serving dish, keep warm while finishing sauce.

Pour the liquid into a clean pan and boil rapidly until reduced by half.

Cream the remaining butter with the flour, then, using a balloon whisk, whisk small knobs of the butter and flour into the liquid. Cook, whisking throughout until the sauce is thick. Add remaining parsley with cream and season.

Pour over mussels and serve immediately with crusty bread and a glass of white wine.

HANDY TIP

Mussels are highly nutritious, rich in mineral salts, iron, vitamins A,B,C,D and protein, but they need to be bought and eaten the same day, as they quickly go bad.

1. Place mussels in plenty of salted water. Scrub to remove dirt

2. Using a small, sharp knife, scrape off barnacles and discard beards

3. Sauté the shallots and garlic, add wine, stock, bay leaves and remaining herbs

4. Add mussels to the liquid a few at a time. Cover with a close-fitting lid

5. Pull mussels apart, discarding top shells, and keep warm while making sauce

6. Whisk the butter-and-flour paste, in small knobs, into the boiling liquid

DRESSED CRAB

This impressive dish is ideal for a light summer's lunch, served with a selection of salads and a glass of chilled white wine, or as a starter for a dinner party. And just because it looks impressive don't think it's difficult to make.

Calories per portion: 254

SERVES 4

2 crabs, approx 1½ lb/675 g
   each, cooked

2 eggs, size 5

salt and freshly ground
   black pepper

1 oz/25 g fresh brown
   breadcrumbs

juice of 1 lemon

curly endive to garnish

Crabs are normally sold ready cooked but when buying, test the weight of them in relation to their size. Avoid any that feel light, as this may mean they have recently shed their shells and have little flesh.

Wash the crab well under cold running water before starting. This prevents any pieces of dirt getting into

the flesh. When preparing the crab, place shell upside down on a work surface with the underside facing you. Then remove the claws from the body by twisting against the direction the large claws or pincers are facing, followed by the eight legs. Reserve.

To open the shell twist off the bony tail, then insert a sharp, rigid knife between the main shell and underside. Twist and pull them apart. From the underside piece, discard the dead men's fingers or gills (these are soft greyish and elongated). Then discard the stomach sac which is bag-like and slightly furry. The rest of the crab flesh is edible.

Cut the underside portion in half then using a skewer, prise out the white flesh from all the crevices. Place in a bowl. Then take the shell and scoop out the dark meat, keeping it separate from the white meat. If the crab has a lot of roe this can be mixed in with the dark meat.

Using a rolling pin gently crack open the large pincers, extract the meat with a skewer and flake finely. Put with rest of white meat.

Around the empty shell you'll notice a thin line running about ¼ in/6 mm from the edge. Using the handle of a wooden spoon or the tip of a rolling pin, carefully tap to remove the thin shell outside the groove. Wash the shell and oil lightly. Reserve.

Meanwhile, boil the eggs for 10 mins, plunge in to cold water, then leave until cold. Flake the white crab flesh and mix with salt and pepper to taste. Mix the brown breadcrumbs into the dark meat with 1-2 tbsp lemon juice.

Arrange the white flesh into each

HANDY TIP

Keep the shells afterwards as they make attractive dishes for starters. Wash well after each use.

---

side of the cleaned shells with the dark meat in the centre. Remove shells from eggs, sieve yolk and finely chop white. Arrange in straight lines in between the dark and white meat.

Place on serving platter and garnish with endive. Carefully arrange the smaller claws around it and then decorate with lemon twists. Serve with thinly sliced brown bread and butter.

1. Place the crab, shell side down, flat on a board, then carefully twist off the claws or pincers, then the legs

2. Insert a sharp, strong knife between main shell and underside, twist then pull free

3. Discard dead men's fingers or gills (shown left on board) from underside of crab

4. Discard stomach sac, cut underside in half, using a skewer prise out flesh

5. Scoop out the dark meat from the shell and keep separate from the white

6. Crack the larger claws with a clean rolling pin and extract all the meat

FISH TERRINE

Such a variety of fish goes into this delicious dish! Sumptuous smoked salmon tops off everyday cod, haddock and prawns in a rich sauce to create a terrine that's tempting, tasty and terrific! Serve it up and you won't need to fish for compliments.

Calories per portion: 486   **SERVES 6**

10 oz/300 g thinly sliced
   smoked salmon
8 oz/225 g cod fillet, skinned
8 oz/225 g smoked haddock
   fillet, skinned
1 pint/600 ml milk
1 small onion, peeled
1 small carrot, peeled and sliced
1 celery stick, trimmed and sliced
2 fresh bay leaves
1 oz/25 g butter or margarine
1 oz/25 g flour
salt and freshly ground
   white pepper
6 oz/175 g peeled prawns, thawed
   if frozen
1 tbsp tomato purée
1 tbsp freshly chopped dill
½ oz/15 g gelatine
½ pint/300 ml whipping cream
salad leaves, sliced lemon and
   fresh dill sprigs to garnish

Cut out a thin circle of greaseproof paper that will sit in the base of a 2 pint/1.2 litre ring mould. Lightly oil the mould, place the greaseproof in the base and brush with oil.

Line the prepared mould with smoked salmon, overlapping slices slightly and allowing a little to hang over the edge. Cover and leave in fridge while preparing the filling.

Wash and pat dry the cod and haddock. Place the cod in a large frying pan with ½ pint/300 ml milk, the onion, carrot, celery and bay leaves, then poach gently for 10-12 mins, or until the fish is cooked. Remove cod from the pan and leave to cool. Add the smoked haddock to the pan, topping up with a little water if necessary, and poach for 10-12 mins, or until cooked. Drain and allow to cool. Discard the milk and the vegetables.

When fillets are cool, flake with a fork. Melt fat in a small pan, add flour and cook for 2 mins. Draw off the heat and gradually stir in the remaining milk. Return to the heat and cook, stirring throughout, until the sauce thickens. Remove from the heat and season to taste. Place the fish in two separate bowls, then divide two thirds of the sauce equally between each. Add prawns and tomato purée to the remaining sauce in pan. Add the chopped dill to the cod. Mix well.

Dissolve the gelatine in 6 tbsp very hot water, then carefully stir 2 tbsp into each of the mixtures.

Whip cream until soft peaks are formed, then stir equal amounts into each mixture. Spoon the prawn mixture into the base of the lined mould, then the cod, and finally the smoked haddock, smoothing the top of each as you go.

Bring the overhanging smoked salmon over the top to cover the mixture completely. Leave in the fridge for at least 2 hrs, or until set. When set, carefully loosen, then serve, garnished with salad leaves, lemon slices and fresh dill sprigs.

HANDY TIP

The terrine can be made in advance and frozen. Allow to thaw overnight in the fridge.

1. Cut out a circle of greaseproof paper and place in a lightly greased ring mould

2. Line the lightly greased mould with overlapping thin slices of smoked salmon

3. Separate haddock and cod, and add sauce. Mix prawns with remaining sauce

4. Dissolve the gelatine in hot water, then stir 2 tbsp into each separate mixture

5. Layer the three fish mixtures into the mould, finishing with the haddock

6. Smooth the surface of the mixture, carefully fold the smoked salmon over

CHEESE SOUFFLE

Does your heart sink when you think of making a soufflé? Follow this step-by-step guide and it will turn out perfect every time. It really is as light as a feather – and great for supper or as a starter for a dinner party.

2 oz/50 g butter or margarine

2 oz/50 g flour

7 fl oz/200 ml milk, warmed

4 eggs, size 3, separated

salt and freshly ground
   black pepper

4 oz/100 g mature Cheddar
   cheese, finely grated

1 tsp ready-made
   mustard, optional

Set oven to Gas 4, 350°F, 180°C, and place a baking sheet in the oven to heat through. (Putting the soufflé on to a hot baking sheet will help it to rise.) Lightly grease a 6 in/15 cm soufflé dish.

Melt the butter or margarine in a saucepan, stir in the flour and cook for

2 mins until the mixture forms a ball in the centre of the pan. Remove from the heat and gradually stir in the milk, beating well between each addition. Return the pan to the heat and cook for 3 mins, stirring throughout or until the mixture thickens.

Allow to cool slightly, add the egg yolks one at a time, beating well between each addition. Add seasoning, cheese and mustard, if using.

Whisk egg whites with a pinch of salt until stiff and standing in peaks, carefully fold into the cheese mixture. Pour the mixture into the soufflé dish and place in the oven on the hot baking sheet. Cook for 50-60 mins or until well risen and golden brown. Serve immediately.

HANDY TIP

Once you've tried and enjoyed a cheese soufflé, ring the changes by varying the ingredients. Keep the method the same, but omit the cheese and instead add to the cooked white sauce 4 oz/100 g cooked finely-flaked smoked cod or haddock from which you have discarded all the bones and skin, with 1 tbsp freshly chopped parsley. Or try replacing 2 oz/50 g of the cheese with 3 oz/75 g cooked and finely chopped mushrooms which have been thoroughly drained.

1. Melt butter in the pan, stir in flour and cook over a gentle heat

2. Gradually add the milk, beating well between each addition until thickened

3. Cool slightly, add egg yolks one at a time, then add cheese and seasoning

4. Whisk egg whites until stiff and standing in peaks – a pinch of salt helps

5. Fold egg whites into the cooled mixture a little at a time. Do not over mix

6. Spoon mixture into greased soufflé dish and lightly tap the dish to level top

CHICKEN GUMBO

Spice up your meal-times with this delicious Cajun dish, full of tender chicken, sausages and vegetables, and seasoned with chillis, Tabasco, paprika and ground peppers. Serve it with rice to soak up the sauce and treat the family to a tasty change.

Calories per portion: 735   **SERVES 8**

2 x 2 lb/900 g corn-fed oven-ready chickens

3½ tsp salt

2 tsp paprika pepper

2 tsp freshly ground black pepper

1½ tsp freshly ground white pepper

5 tbsp oil

2 onions

2 red peppers

2-4 chillis (amount depends on how hot you like your food)

3 sticks of celery

8 oz/225 g okra

2 tbsp flour or filé powder

4 pints/2.25 litres chicken stock

3 smoked pork sausages or Italian or Spanish sausages

1 bunch of spring onions

¼-½ tsp Tabasco sauce

1 tbsp freshly chopped parsley

8 oz/225 g long-grain rice, freshly cooked

HANDY TIPS

Gumbos vary from area to area and there is no hard and fast rule – you can vary the ingredients according to personal taste and availability of produce.
Many gumbos contain okra, but you can still make it without them. Filé powder is a Cajun thickening agent.

Wash and dry the chickens, then, using a large sharp knife, cut each one into eight portions. Wash and dry again. Mix together salt and peppers, sprinkle half over the chicken portions. Reserve the remainder.

Heat 4 tbsp oil in a frying pan, sauté the chicken in batches until browned, then drain on kitchen paper. Peel and finely chop onions. Deseed the peppers and chillis, and chop finely. Trim, wash and chop the celery and okra.

Heat the remaining oil in a pan, then sauté half of the prepared vegetables for 10 mins, or until they are softened. Sprinkle in the flour or filé powder and cook gently for a further 15 mins, or until the mixture is golden brown. Reserve.

Place the stock and remaining prepared vegetables in a large saucepan, bring to the boil, then stir in remaining salt and peppers mixture. Cut sausages into chunks, then add to the saucepan with the browned chicken and simmer gently for 1½ hrs. Add the reserved vegetables and cook for a further 25 mins. Skim off any fat that rises to the surface. Trim, wash and chop the spring onions, then add to the saucepan with Tabasco sauce to taste. Cook for 10-15 mins.

Transfer the gumbo to a serving dish or tureen and sprinkle with chopped parsley. Divide freshly cooked rice equally between individual serving dishes and spoon the chicken gumbo over the top of each. Serve with freshly baked corn or crusty bread.

1. Wash and dry chickens, then, using a sharp knife, cut each into eight portions

2. Mix together salt and peppers, sprinkle half over chicken portions and sauté

3. Peel and chop onions. Chop peppers, chillis and prepared celery and okra

4. *Place stock and half the vegetables in a pan, stir in reserved seasonings*

5. *Add the sausages and chicken to the pan, then simmer gently for 1½ hrs*

6. *Add reserved vegetables to pan, cook for a further 25 mins, then skim off fat*

CRAB CAKES

Serve these delicious fish cakes any day of the week and give the whole family a real treat! Made from mouthwatering, succulent crab meat and subtly flavoured with mustard and Tabasco, they're so tasty and really quick and easy to prepare.

Calories per portion: 627

SERVES 4

½ oz/15 g butter or margarine

½ oz/15 g plain flour

¼ pint/150 ml milk

1 lb/450 g white crab meat,
    thoroughly drained

1 tsp dry mustard

1 small onion, peeled and
    finely chopped

dash of Tabasco

1 tbsp freshly chopped parsley

6 tbsp fresh white breadcrumbs

1 tbsp reduced-calorie
    mayonnaise

salt and freshly ground
    black pepper

4 tbsp dry breadcrumbs or plain
    flour for coating

1 oz/25 g butter or margarine

2 tbsp sunflower oil

few fresh parsley sprigs to garnish

FOR THE DRESSING:

¼ pint/150 ml reduced-calorie
    mayonnaise

3 tbsp low-fat natural yogurt

1 tbsp freshly chopped parsley

grated rind of 1 lemon

2 tsp wholegrain mustard

Melt the fat in the pan, then add the flour and cook for 2 mins. Draw pan off the heat and gradually blend in milk. Return pan to heat and cook, stirring, until the sauce has thickened. Set to one side, covered with a sheet of damp greaseproof paper. Leave until cool.

Place the crab meat in a bowl, flake, then add sauce, together with the mustard, onion, Tabasco and parsley. Stir in the fresh breadcrumbs and enough mayonnaise to form a stiff but pliable mixture. Season, then cover and chill for 30 mins. Lightly dust a board and your hands with flour, divide the mixture into eight equal portions and shape into flat cakes.

Coat the crab cakes in the dried

breadcrumbs or flour and lightly press into the surface, ensuring the cakes are thoroughly coated. Chill in the fridge for about 30 mins. Meanwhile, make the dressing by mixing all the ingredients together until thoroughly blended.

Heat the butter or margarine and oil in a frying pan, then fry the cakes for 4-5 mins on each side, or until golden and crispy and thoroughly heated

HANDY TIP

Try adding one small peeled and grated onion and one small deseeded, chopped green pepper for extra crunch.

through. Drain on absorbent kitchen paper and serve immediately, garnished with parsley, and with the dressing.

1. Melt fat in the pan, add flour and cook for 2 mins, then gradually blend in milk

2. Flake crab meat. Add sauce with the mustard, onion, Tabasco and parsley

3. Stir in breadcrumbs and mayonnaise to form a firm, pliable mixture. Season

4. Dust board and hands with flour, divide mixture into eight and shape into cakes

5. Coat the crab cakes in the dried breadcrumbs or flour, then chill for 30 mins

6. To make the dressing, mix all the ingredients together until blended

BEEFBURGERS

Give the kids a treat with these delicious home-made beefburgers. By preparing the beef yourself, you can guarantee they are lean – and, served with our chilli'n'tomato ketchup, they're great.

FOR THE CHILLI'N'TOMATO KETCHUP:

- 1 small onion
- 1 garlic clove
- 8 oz/225 g ripe tomatoes
- ½ green pepper
- 1-2 red chillis
- 1 tbsp tomato purée
- 1 tbsp white wine vinegar
- 1 tsp ground cloves
- 1 tbsp clear honey

FOR THE BURGERS:

- 1 lb/450 g lean beef, such as topside
- 2 onions
- 1 egg, size 3, beaten
- salt and freshly ground black pepper
- 2 tbsp oil
- 4 baps
- few lettuce leaves

Preheat the grill 10 mins before grilling the burgers. To make the chilli'n'tomato ketchup, peel and finely chop the onion, then peel and crush the garlic clove. Peel the tomatoes, then deseed and chop roughly. Deseed and finely chop the green pepper.

Place chopped onion, garlic,

HANDY TIP

Make burgers and cook as above, then top with one slice of drained pineapple and one slice of cheese, cook under preheated grill until golden brown.

---

tomatoes and pepper in a small pan. Deseed the chillis and chop finely. (When handling the chillis, take care not to touch your face – especially your eyes and mouth. Wash hands thoroughly after preparing the chillis.) Add the chillis, tomato purée, vinegar and cloves to the pan, then place over a gentle heat and stir in the honey. Bring to the boil, then reduce the heat, cover and leave to simmer gently for 40 mins, or until mixture forms the consistency of chutney.

Meanwhile, prepare the beefburgers. Trim beef, discarding any fat or gristle. Cut meat into thick strips, then dice into small pieces. Using two large sharp knives, and working the knives as though you are beating a drum, chop meat finely (alternatively, pass it through a mincer). Peel and chop one onion, place in a mixing bowl and add meat and beaten egg. Season to taste. Mix well, then, using your hands, shape into burgers (you may find it easier if your hands are slightly wet).

Lightly brush the burgers with a little oil, cook under a preheated grill for 3-4 mins, or until sealed. Turn burgers over, brush again with a little oil and grill for 3 mins. Continue to cook the burgers for 5-6 mins, or until cooked.

Peel and slice the remaining onion, fry gently in remaining oil for 5-8 mins. Drain. Split baps in half and toast lightly.

Sandwich lettuce, cooked burgers, onion and a little ketchup between the baps. Serve with remaining ketchup, chips, dill cucumbers and coleslaw.

1. Place onion, garlic, tomatoes and pepper in pan. Deseed and chop chillis

2. Place pan over a gentle heat, stir in honey. Reduce heat, cover and simmer

3. Trim beef, discarding any fat or gristle, cut the meat into thick strips and dice

4. Using two sharp knives, work them as though beating a drum, chop meat

5. Place the chopped onion and the prepared meat in a mixing bowl. Season

6. Using slightly wet hands, shape the minced beef into burgers before grilling

ONION TART

Deliciously crisp, light pastry, sweet-tasting onions and a rich creamy filling flavoured with Gruyère cheese, make this great French dish the ideal light lunch or supper for all the family. Serve it hot or cold with a fresh mixed salad and crusty bread.

Calories per portion: 328   **SERVES 8**

FOR THE PASTRY:
8 oz/225 g plain white flour
pinch of salt
2 oz/50 g butter or margarine
2 oz/50 g white vegetable fat
FOR THE FILLING:
12 oz/350 g onions
1 bunch of spring onions
1 oz/25 g butter or margarine
3 eggs, size 3
¼ pint/150 ml single cream
salt and freshly ground
**   black pepper**
1 oz/25 g Gruyère cheese

Preheat the oven to Gas 6, 400°F, 200°C, 15 mins before baking the pastry. Sieve the flour and salt into a mixing bowl. Cut the fats into small cubes and add to the bowl. Using your fingertips, lightly rub the fats into the flour until the mixture resembles fine breadcrumbs. Mix to a firm but pliable dough with about 4 tbsp cold water. Turn out of bowl and knead lightly on a floured surface until the pastry is smooth and free of any cracks. Wrap in greaseproof paper and chill in the fridge for 30 mins.

Roll the chilled pastry out on a lightly floured surface and, using the rolling pin to help you lift it, line a 9 in/23 cm loose-bottomed flan or quiche tin. Roll the pin across top to remove any excess pastry. Place a sheet of tin foil over the pastry, then cover with baking beans and bake blind in the oven for 10 mins.

Remove paper and beans from the pastry case and continue to cook for a further 5 mins. Remove from oven, then reduce oven temperature to Gas 4, 350°F, 180°C.

Peel and thinly slice the onions. Trim, wash and chop the spring onions. Melt the fat in a frying pan, then gently sauté

HANDY TIP

As an alternative, try using 8 oz/225 g leeks instead of the spring onions, adding 4 oz/100 g streaky bacon, derinded and chopped, to the onions.

the onions for 8-10 mins, or until soft and transparent. Add the spring onions and continue to cook for a further 2 mins. Drain well, then arrange in the cooked pastry case.

Beat together the eggs, cream and seasoning, then pour over the onions. Finely grate the cheese and sprinkle over the top, then return the tart to the oven. Cook for 25-30 mins, or until the filling has set and the pastry is a golden brown.

Serve hot or cold with some extra grated cheese, crusty bread and a mixed salad.

1. Chill the prepared pastry for 30 mins in the fridge. Roll out the pastry then, using the rolling pin to help lift it, line the tin

2. Roll the pin across the top to remove any excess pastry, then cover with tin foil and baking beans, bake blind

3. Peel and thinly slice the onions. Trim the spring onions, then wash and chop them

4. Melt fat in frying pan then gently sauté onions and spring onions, drain well, then arrange in cooked pastry case

5. Beat together the eggs, cream and seasoning, then gently pour over the cooked onions

6. Finely grate the cheese, sprinkle over the top and cook until filling has set and the pastry is golden

BUBBLE & SQUEAK

Dish up an all-time favourite with this classic recipe that uses up the Sunday roast dinner in the tastiest of ways. Simply fry the meat and veg, or choose our vegetable-only version, for a truly mouthwatering supper.

Calories per portion: 431   SERVES 2

6 slices cold, cooked roast beef

1 medium onion

2 oz/50 g butter or dripping

6 oz/175 g leftover
   cooked cabbage

8 oz/225 g leftover
   mashed potatoes

1 tbsp creamed horseradish

salt and freshly ground
   black pepper

Discard any fat and gristle from the roast beef, cut into bite-sized pieces. Peel and finely chop the onion. Melt butter or dripping in a frying pan, then fry onion for 8-10 mins, or until golden.

Meanwhile, finely chop cooked cabbage, discarding any that is very overcooked. Mash potatoes again to ensure they are smooth.

Add the beef to the fried onion in the pan, continue to fry for 5 mins, then spoon in the potatoes. Next, add the chopped cabbage and the creamed horseradish. Season with the salt and ground black pepper and stir well.

Cook over a moderate heat, stirring throughout, and pressing the mixture down into the pan with the back of a wooden spatula for about 2 mins, or until the base of the mixture is golden brown and piping hot. Serve immediately with fresh crusty bread and salad.

(If liked, add other leftover vegetables to the pan, such as brussel sprouts, mashed swede or peas, and use lamb instead of beef if preferred.)

HANDY TIPS

VEGETARIAN BUBBLE & SQUEAK

Serves 4
Calories per portion: 400

I onion
I garlic clove
2 oz/50 g polyunsaturated
margarine
8 oz/225 g cooked
potatoes, mashed
4 oz/100 g cooked carrots
6 oz/175 g cooked cabbage
3 oz/75 g shelled Brazil
nuts, chopped
2 oz/50 g unsalted cashew nuts
2 oz/50 g sunflower or
pumpkin seeds
salt and freshly ground
black pepper

Peel and chop onion. Peel and
crush garlic. Melt margarine
in a frying pan and cook onion
and garlic for 8-10 mins until
golden. Re-mash potatoes
until smooth, and roughly chop
the carrots and cabbage.
Add potatoes, carrots and
cabbage to pan and mix well.
Stir in the nuts and sunflower
or pumpkin seeds. Season and
cook for 20 mins, or until the
base of the mixture is golden
brown and piping hot.
Serve immediately.

For a change, prepare the
Bubble & Squeak as directed, but
remove from the heat and allow
to cool after seasoning. Shape
into 6-8 cakes, brush with a little
oil and cook in a preheated oven,
Gas 6, 400°F, 200°C, for 15 mins
or until piping hot.

I. Discard any fat or gristle from the cold roast beef, then cut into bite-sized pieces. Cover and reserve

3. Meanwhile, finely chop cooked cabbage, discarding any that is very overcooked. Remash potatoes

5. Spoon the cold mashed potatoes on top of the fried onion and beef in the pan

2. Peel and finely chop the onion, then fry in the butter or dripping for 8-10 mins, or until golden

4. Add the roast beef pieces to the fried onion in the pan. Continue to fry for 5 mins mixing well together

6. Add the chopped cabbage, together with horseradish. Season and stir well

CHICKEN RISOTTO

Succulent chunks of chicken, sweet red and green peppers, tender mushrooms... all mixed into lots of light and tasty rice. This risotto is delicious and so easy to cook, too. It's the perfect dish to serve as a supper-time treat for all the family.

Calories per portion: 516   **SERVES 4**

2 medium onions
1-2 garlic cloves
2 celery sticks
1 red pepper
1 green pepper
4 oz/100 g button mushrooms
4 tbsp olive oil
10 oz/300 g Arborio (risotto) rice
1¼ pint/750 ml chicken stock
1 lb/450 g cooked chicken meat
½ oz/15 g unsalted butter
salt and freshly ground
     black pepper
juice of ½ lemon
2 tbsp freshly chopped tarragon
tarragon sprig to garnish

Peel and finely chop the onions, peel and crush the garlic. Trim and scrub the celery sticks, then chop. Wash the peppers, and cut in half. Remove and discard the stems, seeds and pithy white flesh from inside the peppers, then chop the flesh. Wash or wipe the mushrooms, then slice; reserve.

Heat 3 tbsp olive oil in a flameproof pan or a large frying pan, then gently sauté the chopped onions, garlic and celery for 5 mins, or until the vegetables are soft and transparent. Sprinkle in the rice and continue to sauté for a further 2 mins. Add the chopped peppers and cook for a further 2 mins. Pour the chicken stock into the pan and bring to the boil. Stir, then reduce the heat and simmer gently for 15 mins, stirring mixture occasionally with a wooden spoon or spatula.

Meanwhile, chop the chicken meat into bite-sized pieces. Add the chopped chicken to the pan, stir the mixture thoroughly, then continue to cook for a further 15 mins, stirring occasionally.

In a small pan, melt the butter with the remaining olive oil, then gently cook the sliced mushrooms for 1-2 mins, or until just sealed. Add mushrooms to the risotto with the salt, ground black pepper and lemon juice.

Continue to cook the risotto for a further 5 mins to ensure that the rice is fully cooked and the chicken is thoroughly heated through. (You can add a little extra stock at this stage, if necessary.)

Sprinkle in the freshly chopped tarragon, stir, then serve immediately, garnished with the tarragon sprig.

Serve with grated Parmesan cheese if desired, and a crisp green salad and crusty bread.

HANDY TIP

A cooked 2½ lb/1.25 kg chicken should give you approximately 1 lb/450 g meat once you have removed the skin and bones.

1. Peel and finely chop the onions, peel and crush the garlic, trim, wash and chop the celery

2. Cut peppers in half, discard stems, seeds and white pith, then chop. Wipe or wash the mushrooms, then slice

3. Sauté the onions, garlic and celery in the oil for 5 mins, or until the vegetables are soft. Sprinkle in the rice

4. Add the chopped peppers to the pan and continue to sauté mixture for 2 more mins

5. Pour in the chicken stock and bring to the boil. Reduce heat, then simmer gently for 15 mins

6. Chop the cooked chicken meat into bite-sized pieces, add to the pan, stir and continue to cook for a further 15 mins

TORTELLONI

Treat them to a classic taste of Italy with this delicious pasta dish. Filled with spinach and cheese, then covered with a super, fresh tomato sauce, it's a main meal the whole family will love – and it's perfect for vegetarians, too.

Calories per portion: 948   **SERVES 4**

FOR THE PASTA DOUGH:

1 lb/450 g strong plain flour

½ tsp salt

6 eggs, size 1

2-3 tbsp olive oil

FOR THE SPINACH FILLING:

1 garlic clove, peeled and crushed

12 oz/350 g fresh spinach, prepared, cooked and finely chopped

6 oz/175 g ricotta cheese

1½ oz/40 g Parmesan cheese, grated

2 eggs, size 5

salt and freshly ground black pepper

1 tsp grated nutmeg

FOR THE TOMATO SAUCE:

1 lb/450 g ripe tomatoes

2 tbsp olive oil

1 onion, peeled and chopped

1 garlic clove, peeled and crushed

2 sticks celery, trimmed and finely chopped

2 tbsp tomato purée

basil sprigs

¼ pint/150 ml white wine or vegetable stock

1 tbsp cornflour

To make the pasta dough, place the flour on a clean working surface, make a well in the centre and add the salt, eggs and olive oil. Gradually mix the flour into the eggs and oil until the mixture forms a stiff but pliable dough, then knead until smooth and elastic. This will take about 5-10 mins. Cover with a clean cloth and leave to relax for

1 hr. Meanwhile, mix together filling ingredients in a large bowl and leave covered until ready to use.

To make the sauce, peel the tomatoes then chop roughly. Heat the oil, then sauté onion, garlic and celery for 5 mins. Add chopped tomatoes and cook for a further 10 mins. Stir in the tomato purée, basil (reserving a few sprigs for garnishing), and wine or stock. Season. Cook for a further 10 mins. Pass through a blender until smooth, then return to the rinsed pan. Just before using, blend the cornflour with 2 tbsp water, stir into sauce. Heat until thickened. Keep warm.

To prepare the tortelli, thinly roll out the pasta dough and cut out 2½ in/6.5 cm circles. Place 1 tsp prepared spinach filling in the centre of each pasta circle. Dampen edges, then fold over to form a half-moon. Gently curve each piece into a ring and pinch ends together, ensuring shape remains curled. Lay the tortelli apart on a clean, lightly floured tea towel. Leave to dry for a few minutes.

Cook the pasta in boiling, salted water for 5 mins, or until cooked. Drain well. Mix into the prepared tomato sauce, then serve right away with a side salad, garnished with reserved basil.

HANDY TIP

Add 1 tsp of olive oil to the water when cooking the tortelli to prevent them sticking together.

1. Mix together all the filling ingredients, then leave covered until ready to use

2. Carefully cut out 2½ in/6.5 cm circles from the thinly rolled-out pasta dough

3. Place 1 tsp prepared spinach filling in the centre of each pasta circle

4. Dampen edges of pasta, then fold to form a half-moon shape. Pinch edges

5. Gently curve each pasta piece into a ring until the two ends are touching

6. Pinch the ends firmly together, then leave to dry on a clean tea towel

KEDGEREE

Moist, succulent chunks of salmon and smoked haddock, gently poached in white wine and herbs, then mixed with rice and lightly sautéed onion. Kedgeree is a delicious dish, ideal for an informal supper, brunch, or as a starter.

Calories per portion: 382

SERVES 6

2 eggs, size 3

6 oz/175 g long-grain rice

1 salmon tail, approx 1 lb/450 g
    in weight

few parsley stalks

2-3 bay leaves

2 onions, peeled

¼ pint/150 ml white wine or
    fish stock

8 oz/225 g undyed
    smoked haddock

4 oz/100 g butter

1-2 tsp curry powder, or
    to taste

salt and freshly ground
    black pepper

sprigs of fresh coriander or
    parsley to garnish

Allow the eggs to stand at room temperature for 30 mins. Bring a pan of water to the boil, then gently place the eggs into the water. Bring back to the boil, then cook eggs gently for 10 mins. Remove from the heat, drain, then place under cold running water. Leave in cold water until required.

Cook the rice in a saucepan of fast boiling salted water for 12-15 mins, or until just cooked. Drain and rinse under cold water. Reserve.

Descale the salmon and wash thoroughly. Place in a frying pan with the parsley stalks and bay leaves. Slice one onion, add to pan, pour in the white wine or stock and ½ pint/300 ml water. Bring to the boil, cover, then simmer gently for 10 mins, or until the fish is cooked. Remove from the pan and drain, reserving cooking liquid.

Wash smoked haddock, place in clean frying pan with more parsley stalks, bay leaves and the reserved liquid. Cook as before for 10 mins. Drain. When the salmon and haddock are cool enough to handle, discard the skin and bones and flake the flesh into large chunks.

Melt the butter in a clean pan. Peel and finely chop remaining onion, then cook in the melted butter for 5 mins. Add curry powder and cook for 2 mins. Add reserved rice and chunks of fish.

Heat through, stirring until piping hot. Shell the hard-boiled eggs and slice thinly. Add to the kedgeree, with salt and pepper to taste. Stir well, then pile kedgeree on to a warmed serving dish and garnish with sprigs of fresh coriander or parsley. Serve hot.

HANDY TIPS

You can vary the fish according to your budget and, if you prefer, you can use just one type of fish. Remember that fish doesn't keep for very long, so if necessary, freeze it straight after buying it (as long as it hasn't been frozen before) and thaw just before using. Never keep cooked fish – it should always be used on the day it's cooked.

1. Cook rice in boiling salted water, drain, rinse under cold water. Reserve

2. Poach salmon in wine and water with parsley, bay leaves and onion for 10 mins

3. Fry the chopped onion in melted butter for 5 mins. Stir in curry powder

4. Remove the salmon skin, remove flesh from bones, flake into large chunks

5. Add the flaked, cooked, smoked haddock to rice and mix thoroughly

6. Mix in salmon, add salt and freshly ground pepper. Heat thoroughly

SPANISH OMELETTE

This version has got to be the most famous of all omelettes... using mainly potato and onion, it's so tasty and filling. Serve it tapas style in small squares for a super family snack, or make a meal of it with salad and crusty bread.

Calories per portion: 172   SERVES 6

1 lb/450 g potatoes

2 red peppers

1 green pepper

1 large Spanish onion

2-3 garlic cloves

12 oz/350 g ripe tomatoes

2-3 tbsp olive oil

8 eggs, size 3

salt and freshly ground
   black pepper

1 tbsp freshly chopped oregano

Peel the potatoes then cook them in boiling salted water until tender. Drain well and reserve.

Wash and dry the peppers, trim the tops, discard seeds and the membrane inside. Slice thinly, place in boiling water for 3 mins, drain and reserve. Peel the onion, slice thinly. Peel and then crush the garlic cloves.

Make a small cross on the stalk end of each tomato, place in a small bowl, cover with boiling water, leave for 2 mins, drain then skin. Cut each tomato into quarters, discard the core and seeds, then chop and reserve.

Heat olive oil in a large, heavy-based frying pan. Add the sliced onion and crushed garlic, then fry gently, stirring frequently until the onions are soft and transparent and just beginning to turn golden.

Dice the cooled potatoes into

¼ in/6 mm cubes. Add to the frying pan with the reserved, blanched peppers, and continue to cook for a further 2 mins. Stir in the chopped, skinned tomatoes.

Beat the eggs with 2 tbsp cold water and salt and pepper. Pour into the pan, then cook for 3-4 mins over a moderately high heat. This will allow the egg to set lightly on the bottom.

Using a spatula gently push the set egg from round the outside edge of the frying pan to the centre. Lower the heat slightly then continue to cook, gently pushing the egg to the centre until it is completely set. As you are gently stirring, make sure that you keep the vegetables evenly distributed throughout the omelette.

Once the omelette is set, place under a preheated grill to lightly brown the top and to ensure that the omelette is completely set in the centre.

Serve cut into wedges sprinkled with the oregano.

HANDY TIPS

While cooking, take care that the heat is not too fierce, otherwise the bottom of the omelette may burn slightly. If liked, Spanish sausage, salchica or chorizo can be diced and added to the omelette, along with the potatoes and peppers. Marjoram may be substituted for the oregano.

1. Wash and dry the peppers, trim the tops, discard insides and slice thinly. Place in boiling water for 3 mins

2. Heat olive oil in a large heavy-based frying pan, add sliced onion and crushed garlic and fry gently

3. Add the cubed potatoes and sliced peppers to the frying pan and cook for a further 2 mins

4. Beat eggs with 2 tbsp water and seasoning. Add to pan and cook for 3-4 mins

5. Lower the heat and push the egg to the centre until it is completely set

6. Once omelette is set, place under a preheated grill to lightly brown top

MEATBALLS WITH SAUCE

Every country adds their own special magic to this well-known dish. This version is an Italian classic, the secret is in the delicious sauce using sun-ripened tomatoes and basil. Serve with cooked pasta.

Calories per portion: 337

SERVES 4

2 garlic cloves

12 oz/350 g ground beef or very lean minced beef

1 medium onion

1 lemon (preferably unwaxed)

2 tbsp freshly chopped parsley

salt and freshly ground black pepper

2 oz/50 g fresh white breadcrumbs

1 egg, size 3, beaten

2-3 tbsp olive oil

FOR THE TOMATO SAUCE:

1 small onion

1 garlic clove

1 lb/450 g ripe tomatoes

¼ pint/150 ml dry white wine or vegetable stock

1-2 tbsp tomato purée

1 tbsp freshly chopped basil

fresh basil sprigs to garnish

Peel and crush the garlic cloves, then add to the ground beef. Place in a large mixing bowl. Peel the onion, chop finely and add to the meat.

Scrub the lemon, dry, then finely grate the rind and add to the meat with the parsley. Season to taste. Mix in breadcrumbs. Add the beaten egg to the meat mixture and work ingredients until they bind together. It is important that the ingredients are evenly distributed throughout, otherwise you will end up with some of the meatballs having too much onion or garlic.

Slightly wet your hands, then place a small spoonful in one hand and shape into a ball, about the size of a large apricot. Place on a plate and continue shaping the mixture into balls until it's all used.

Heat the olive oil in a frying pan, then fry the balls, turning frequently, until cooked through. They should be golden brown and beginning to crisp slightly on the outside. Depending on the size of the meatballs, they will take between 10 and 20 mins to cook. Drain well and place on absorbent paper, before arranging on a serving dish. Keep warm.

Meanwhile, make tomato sauce. Peel the onion and chop finely, Peel and crush the garlic clove. Make a small cross in the top of each tomato, place in a large bowl and pour boiling water over. Leave for 2 mins, drain, peel and discard the skins. Chop roughly, discarding the core.

Place the onion, garlic, chopped tomatoes, and wine or stock in a saucepan. Season to taste. Bring to the boil, then simmer gently, uncovered, for 10 mins, stirring occasionally. Blend the tomato purée with 2-3 tbsp of water and stir into the pan with the freshly chopped basil. Check seasoning and adjust if necessary.

Pour the hot tomato sauce over the meatballs, garnish with sprigs of fresh basil and serve with cooked pasta.

HANDY TIP

Try using ground lamb instead of beef and add 2 tbsp chopped mint.

1. Crush peeled garlic and add to ground beef with finely chopped onion

2. Add the finely grated lemon rind, parsley, seasoning and breadcrumbs

3. Shape the meat mixture into small balls, about the size of an apricot

4. Fry the meat balls in the oil, turning frequently, until golden brown

5. Finely chop peeled onion, crush the garlic, then peel the tomatoes

6. Simmer the tomato sauce ingredients for 10 minutes, or until thickened

PASTIES

Originating in Cornwall, these pasties make a delicious and nutritious snack. Made from tender pieces of meat, potato, carrot and onion, they're encased in a light pastry. Serve hot or cold to satisfy the biggest of appetites.

Calories per portion: 778   SERVES 8

FOR THE PASTRY:

1½ lb/675 g plain white flour

½ tsp salt

6 oz/175 g butter or half-fat
    polyunsaturated margarine

6 oz/175 g white vegetable fat

FOR THE FILLING:

2 sticks celery

6 oz/175 g potatoes

3 oz/75 g carrots

3 oz/75 g turnip or swede

1 oz/25 g butter or margarine

2 tbsp oil

12 oz/350 g braising steak

salt and freshly ground
    black pepper

4 fl oz/120 ml beef or
    vegetable stock

1-2 tsp mixed herbs, optional

1 egg, size 3, beaten

Preheat oven to Gas 6, 400°F, 200°C. Sift flour and salt into mixing bowl then rub in butter or margarine and vegetable fat until mixture resembles fine breadcrumbs. Mix to a soft and pliable dough, with 8 tbsp cold water. Turn the dough out on to a lightly floured surface and knead gently until smooth. Wrap and chill for 30 mins.

Meanwhile, wash the celery and chop into ¼ in/6 mm dice. Peel the potatoes, carrots and turnip or swede. Cut into ¼ in/6 mm dice.

Melt the fat with 1 tbsp oil in a frying pan, and cook the diced vegetables gently for 5-8 mins or until softened but not browned. Drain and reserve.

Trim the steak, discarding any fat or gristle and cut into ½ in/1.25 cm pieces.

Heat remaining oil and fry the meat, stirring occasionally until browned all over. Continue to cook gently for 10 mins. Place the meat in a mixing bowl with vegetables, season to taste.

Moisten with the stock then mix in the herbs if using. Cover the filling and allow to cool completely.

Roll out the pastry on a lightly floured surface and cut into eight 7 in/18 cm circles. Dampen the edges with cold water and place 2 tbsp of the prepared filling in the centre of each circle. Fold over in a half moon shape and pinch edges firmly together. Using the thumb and finger, roll the edge over to give a rope effect.

Place on a lightly greased baking tray and brush with the beaten egg. Bake in the oven for 15 mins then brush again with the egg. Reduce the oven temperature to Gas 4, 350°F, 180°C, and continue to cook for a further 20-25 mins or until golden brown. Serve hot or cold with a selection of vegetables or a salad. These pasties will freeze very well.

HANDY TIP

The rope effect is traditional and comes from olden days when Cornish miners would take their pasties down the mines. In those days the pasties were larger, with a savoury filling at one end and a sweet filling at the other. The miners held the pasty by the rope of pastry to eat and then discarded the rope after eating the pasty. This meant they didn't have to come above ground to wash their hands before eating.

1. Cut vegetables into ¼ in/6 mm dice, then fry in oil and butter for 5-8 mins

2. Cut the steak into ½ in/1.25 cm pieces and fry in the oil until browned

3. Roll pastry out on a lightly floured surface, cut out eight 7 in/18 cm circles

4. Dampen edges of circles and place 2 tbsp of prepared filling in the centre

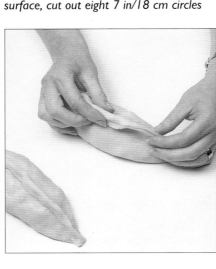

5. Pinch edges together. Using forefinger and thumb, roll edge for rope effect

6. Brush pasties with egg. Bake, brushing with egg halfway through cooking

FISHCAKES

Succulent flakes of fish mixed with creamy mashed potatoes and subtly flavoured with lemon and coriander. Served with mixed vegetables, they make a delicious and nourishing supper dish that the whole family will enjoy.

Calories per portion: 249

1½ lb/675 g fresh fish fillets, such as undyed smoked haddock, cod or whiting

½ pint/300 ml semi-skimmed milk

2 bay leaves

1 medium lemon

1½ lb/675 g potatoes

1 oz/25 g butter or margarine

salt and freshly ground black pepper

1 tsp anchovy essence

1 tbsp freshly chopped coriander or parsley

2 eggs, size 3

4 oz/100 g fresh white breadcrumbs

oil for shallow frying

TO GARNISH:

lemon slices

fresh coriander sprigs

Wash fish, place in a large frying pan with the milk and bay leaves.

Using a zester or grater, remove rind from the lemon and add to pan. Poach the fish gently for 10 mins, or until cooked. Drain, reserving 2-3 tbsp of the poaching liquid. Allow the fish to cool, then discard skin and bones. Flake flesh.

Meanwhile, peel potatoes, cut into chunks, then cook in boiling salted water for 15 mins, or until soft. Drain, then mash with the fat and enough reserved poaching liquid to form a smooth mash. Season with salt and pepper to taste.

Add the flaked fish to the potato, then the anchovy essence and chopped coriander or parsley. Mix well, cover and chill until cold.

Shape into eight 3 in/7.5 cm wide x 1½ in/4 cm deep fishcakes. It may be easier to dust your hands and the work surface lightly with a little flour to prevent the mixture sticking to your

HANDY TIP

Eat the fishcakes the day they're made. Otherwise, freeze them, interleaved with waxed paper, before frying. Allow to thaw before cooking.

hands or the work surface. Place mixture on a baking sheet and cover, then chill until firm.

Beat the eggs, place in a bowl or shallow dish. Dip the fishcakes first in the egg, then in the breadcrumbs. Ensure fishcakes are completely coated.

Heat the oil in a large frying pan to a depth of about 1 in/2.5cm. Carefully cook the fishcakes, a few at a time, for 4-5 minutes on both sides, or until golden brown, crisp and well cooked. Drain on absorbent kitchen paper.

Garnish the fishcakes with lemon twists and sprigs of fresh coriander. Serve piping hot with mixed vegetables.

1. Place fish in large frying pan with the milk, bay leaves and lemon rind

2. Add the flaked fish flesh to the freshly mashed potatoes and mix well

3. Add the anchovy essence – measure accurately, as it has a strong flavour

4. Shape the fish mixture into eight cakes, each 3 in/7.5 cm wide x 1½ in/4 cm deep

5. Dip chilled fishcakes into beaten egg, then coat in fresh breadcrumbs

6. Shallow fry the fishcakes, a few at a time, for 4-5 mins on each side

SAUSAGE ROLLS

Take golden, light flaky pastry, fill it with tasty sausagemeat and you've got the perfect sausage rolls to make your party a complete success. Serve them hot or cold – either way they're simply delicious.

FOR THE PASTRY:
8 oz/225 g plain flour
pinch of salt
3 oz/75 g butter or margarine
3 oz/75 g white vegetable fat
2 tsp lemon juice
FOR THE FILLING:
2 tbsp fresh parsley
**1 small bunch spring onions,
washed and trimmed**
1 lb/450 g pork sausagemeat
1 egg, size 5, beaten

Preheat oven to Gas 6, 400°F, 200°C. Sift flour and salt into a large mixing bowl. Mix the butter or margarine and white vegetable fat together, then divide into four. Add one quarter to the flour and rub in until the mixture resembles fine breadcrumbs. Add the lemon juice and sufficient cold water to make a pliable dough. Knead until smooth and free from cracks.

Roll out to an oblong 12 in × 4 in/ 30 cm × 10 cm. Dot a second quarter of the blended fat over top of the pastry. Fold the bottom of the pastry to the centre, then the top. Seal edges with rolling pin then give the pastry a half turn. Roll out again to the oblong, repeat the dotting with fat and the folding. Seal edges, wrap, chill for 15 mins.

Repeat the rolling and folding once more then chill for 30 mins.

Chop parsley and spring onions, mix well with sausagemeat. Form into two rolls, 12 in/30 cm long.

Roll out pastry on a floured surface to two oblongs, 12 in × 4 in/30 cm × 10 cm. Place the sausagemeat rolls on top of the pastry. Lightly brush the

edges of the pastry with water then fold over to encase the sausagemeat completely. Pinch edges firmly together, then, with a round-bladed knife, knock edges firmly together, sealing well.

Cut into 1½ in/4 cm pieces with a sharp knife then place on lightly greased baking sheets. Mark the sausage rolls across the top with the sharp knife then brush with the beaten egg. Leave to relax in fridge for 20 mins, cook in oven for 15-20 mins, or until golden brown. Cool rolls on a wire cooling rack.

1. Place the sausagemeat in a bowl, together with the parsley and onions

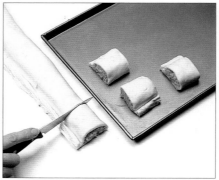

2. Roll out the pastry to an oblong. Form sausagemeat into a long roll

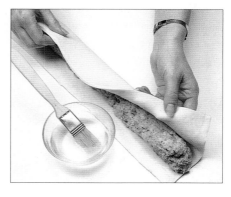

3. Brush edges of pastry with water, fold over to encase sausagemeat

4. Pinch edges then knock together with a knife, sealing well

5. Cut the roll into 1½ in/4 cm pieces then place on a baking sheet

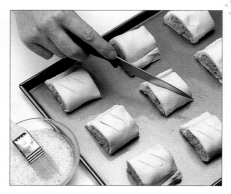

6. Mark the sausage rolls across the top, then brush with beaten egg

STUFFED MARROW

Tender rings of marrow with a lemony, minty lamb filling in a tangy tomato sauce. So full of flavour, this dish is perfect for a family lunch or a supper-time treat. So go on, make the most of marrow and cook a tasty meal.

Calories per portion: 223   **SERVES 4–6**

I marrow about 3 lb/1.5 kg
   in weight
I lemon
I garlic clove
8 oz/225 g finely minced
   lean lamb
I tbsp flour
2 oz/50 g sweetcorn kernels
2 tbsp freshly chopped mint
salt and freshly ground
   black pepper
I lb/450 g ripe tomatoes
2–3 tbsp lamb or
   vegetable stock
I small onion
3 tsp Worcestershire sauce
I tsp golden caster sugar
I tsp arrowroot

Preheat oven to Gas 4, 350°F, 180°C. Thoroughly wash and dry the marrow. Cut into 3 in/7.5 cm rings, then using a small sharp knife, carefully cut round the centre of the rings and remove the pappy flesh and seeds. Discard. Scrub lemon and dry well. Peel and crush garlic clove.

Place the lamb in a large frying pan and dry fry, stirring throughout until the lamb is browned all over. This will help break up the lamb and prevent it

HANDY TIP

Choose marrows that are young and tender. If the marrow is older, you should peel it before stuffing and increase the cooking time slightly.

from forming any lumps.

Add the garlic, flour, sweetcorn and mint, and then season to taste with salt and freshly ground black pepper.

With a lemon zester carefully remove 1 tbsp of lemon rind and add to the mixture.

Peel the tomatoes by making a small cross on the stalk end of the tomato. Plunge into boiling water for 2 mins, then peel. Chop one of the tomatoes, two if they are small, to make 2 tbsp and add to mixture with sufficient stock to moisten. Stir well and cook for a further 5 mins.

Place the prepared marrow rings into a shallow ovenproof dish and fill with the prepared mixture, packing it down firmly.

Place the remaining tomatoes in a food processor or blender and blend to form a smooth purée. Peel the onion and chop, then place in the processor or blender with salt and freshly ground black pepper, the Worcestershire sauce and caster sugar, blend again until smooth.

Pour into a jug and then pour ½ pint/300 ml round the marrow rings.

Cover and cook in the oven for 25-30 mins or until the marrow is cooked and tender.

Heat the remaining sauce with the arrowroot until thick. Arrange the marrow in a serving platter and pour the sauce round. Serve any remaining sauce separately.

Serve the marrow with cooked seasonal vegetables.

1. Wash and dry marrow, cut into 3 in/7.5 cm rings. Prepare lemon and mint

2. With a sharp knife, carefully scoop out seeds and pappy flesh, discard

3. Dry fry the finely minced lamb until browned, stirring to break up the meat

4. After adding garlic, sweetcorn, mint and seasoning, stir in lemon rind

5. Stuff marrow with the prepared mince and place in a shallow ovenproof dish

6. Pour tomato sauce round the stuffed marrow rings, cover then cook in oven

PIZZA MARGHERITA

This pizza has a light crisp base and is topped with tomatoes and basil, creamy mozzarella cheese, anchovies and olives. It's easy to make and ideal for supper or a light lunch for the whole family.

Calories per portion: 585

SERVES 4

1 lb/450 g strong plain white flour

½ tsp salt

½ oz/15 g easy-blend dried yeast

2 tsp sugar

2 tsp oil

14 oz/397 g can chopped tomatoes

1 small onion, peeled and finely grated

1 tbsp freshly chopped basil or 1 tsp dried basil

2 large tomatoes

2 oz/50 g can anchovy fillets

3 tbsp milk

salt and freshly ground black pepper

6 oz/175 g mozzarella cheese, sliced

black olives

few basil leaves to garnish

Preheat oven to Gas 8, 450°F, 230°C, 15 mins before baking pizza. Sift flour and salt in a large mixing bowl. Stir in yeast and sugar. Mix to a soft and pliable dough with ½ pint/300 ml warm water. Knead on a lightly floured surface until smooth. Place in a clean, lightly oiled bowl. Cover with a cloth or clearwrap and leave in a warm place until doubled in size. This will take approx 1 hr.

Turn risen dough onto lightly floured surface and knead again for 5 mins. Roll out to a 9 in/23 cm circle, place on a lightly greased baking sheet. Pinch up edge to form a ½ in/1.25 cm rim.

Purée the canned tomatoes and, if preferred, sieve to remove seeds. Place in bowl with the grated onion and chopped basil. Slice the fresh tomatoes. Soak anchovy fillets in milk for 5 mins.

Spread the puréed tomato mixture over the base and top with the sliced tomato. Season. Arrange the cheese over the tomatoes. Drain the anchovy fillets and arrange in a lattice over the cheese and top with olives.

Bake in oven for 20-25 mins or until the pizza crust is golden, and cheese melted and bubbly. Garnish with basil leaves. Cut into wedges, serve immediately with a tossed salad and a red Italian wine like Chianti Classico.

1. Sift flour into bowl, add salt, yeast and sugar, mix to a dough with water and oil

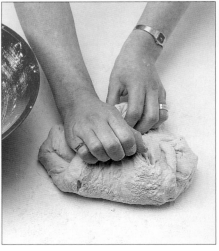

2. Knead dough on lightly floured surface until smooth and pliable. Leave to rest

3. When risen, knead, then roll out on lightly floured surface to 9 in/23 cm round

4. Place on lightly greased baking sheet and pinch up edge to ½ in/1.25 cm

5. Spread puréed tomato over base to ½ in/1.25 cm from edge. Top with tomatoes

6. Arrange sliced mozzarella over tomatoes, then anchovies. Top with olives

PORK STIR-FRY

If you're rushed for time with not a minute to spare and you've got a hungry family to feed, you'll love this tangy sweet and sour Pork Stir-Fry. It's full of succulent meat and crunchy vegetables and takes only minutes to make.

Calories per portion: 513

SERVES 4

3 tbsp sunflower oil

2 oz/50 g piece root ginger,
   peeled and grated

1 lb/450 g pork tenderloin, cut
   into thin strips

2 oz/50 g shallots, peeled

2 small carrots, trimmed and
   peeled, cut into thin strips

½ small red pepper, deseeded and
   cut into thin strips

½ small green pepper, deseeded
   and cut into thin strips

½ small yellow pepper, deseeded
   and cut into thin strips

4 oz/100 g mangetout, trimmed

7 oz/197 g can water chestnuts,
   drained thoroughly

1 small fresh pineapple, peeled,
   cut into chunks or 7 oz/197 g
   can pineapple chunks in natural
   juice (reserve 2-3 tbsp
   of juice)

2-3 tbsp clear honey

2-3 tbsp wine vinegar

2 tbsp soy sauce, or to taste

2 tsp sesame oil

freshly chopped parsley

Heat oil in a wok then quickly fry
grated root ginger for 2 mins. Discard
ginger then add pork and stir fry for
6 mins or until the pork is sealed. Add
shallots, continue stir frying for a further
3 mins to lightly brown the shallots.

When stir frying have the heat fairly
hot and stir continuously so that food
cooks evenly. Continue adding the

HANDY TIPS

Substitute boneless chicken
breasts for the pork. Discard skin
and cut into thin strips.
Or try marinading thin strips of
rump steak in the honey and
vinegar, drain then use as above.

prepared vegetables, leaving pineapple
until last and allowing a couple of
minutes between each addition.

Mix in reserved pineapple juice,
honey, vinegar, then soy sauce.

Heat thoroughly, ensuring that all
ingredients are thoroughly coated. Stir
in sesame oil. Serve immediately with
freshly boiled rice sprinkled with a little
freshly chopped parsley.

1. Using a very sharp knife, carefully slice the pork into 3 in/7.5 cm strips

2. Quickly brown the meat and lightly brown the shallots in hot oil

3. Keep the heat fairly hot, add the strips of carrot and stir fry vigorously

4. Push the cooked ingredients to one side then stir fry the peppers and mangetout

5. Continue stir frying, so that the food is evenly cooked, then add pineapple

6. Add soy sauce, stirring throughout, ensuring all ingredients are coated

MEATLOAF

So simple to make, this dish is delicious served hot with a chunky home-made tomato sauce, jacket baked potato and freshly cooked cabbage, or try it cold with a mixed salad. Either way, it's ideal for lunch or as a supper-time dish.

Calories per portion: 560   SERVES 6

2 onions

2 tbsp oil

I lb/450 g lean minced beef

I lb/450 g lean minced lamb

I-2 garlic cloves

2 tsp paprika pepper

2-3 tbsp freshly chopped mixed
   herbs, such as rosemary,
   oregano and parsley

4 tbsp tomato purée

salt and freshly ground
   black pepper

6 oz/175 g fresh white or brown
   breadcrumbs

2 eggs, size 3

FOR THE TOMATO SAUCE:

I lb/450 g ripe tomatoes

I onion

I tbsp oil

I-2 tbsp tomato
   purée (optional)

¼ pint/150 ml chicken or
   vegetable stock

I tsp sugar

I tbsp freshly chopped basil

salt and freshly ground
   black pepper

Preheat oven to Gas 4, 350°F, 180°C. Peel the onions and chop. Heat the oil in a frying pan then fry the onions for about 5 mins until soft and transparent. Drain well on absorbent kitchen paper and cool.

Place the minced meats into a large bowl then add the cooled, drained onion. Peel and crush the garlic, add to the mixture together with the paprika, chopped fresh herbs, tomato purée,

salt and freshly ground black pepper and breadcrumbs. Mix well together. Beat the eggs then add to mixture. Mix well.

Pack into a 2 lb/900 g loaf tin, packing the mixture well down in the tin, both in the corners and sides of tin.

Cover with tin foil and place in a roasting tin half filled with boiling water. Cook for 1½-2 hrs or until cooked. Uncover for last ½ hr of cooking. (The meatloaf is cooked when the meat starts to shrink away from the sides of the tin.) Allow to cool for 5-10 mins before turning out.

Garnish top of meatloaf with sprigs of fresh herbs.

To make sauce, make a cross at the stalk end of the tomatoes. Place in a large bowl of boiling water. Leave for 2 mins, drain, peel and chop.

Peel onion and roughly chop. Heat the oil in a small pan then fry onion for 5 mins. Add the chopped tomatoes, tomato purée, stock, sugar, basil and seasoning. Cook gently for 10-15 mins or until the sauce is thick. Serve hot with the meatloaf.

If liked use two I lb/450 g loaf tins. Cook for I hr or until cooked. Cool and freeze one for later.

HANDY TIP

The meatloaf is ideal to slice and use in lunch boxes – cool quickly and store for up to two days, well covered, in the fridge.

1. Fry the chopped onion in the oil until soft and transparent, drain well

2. Mix the cooled, drained onion with minced beef and lamb in a large bowl

3. Mix all the other ingredients into the bowl then add beaten egg and stir well

4. Pack the meat mixture into the loaf tin. Press well into the sides and corners

5. Place tomatoes in a bowl of boiling water then peel. Peel onion, chop roughly

6. Just before serving, heat the prepared tomato sauce then season to taste

PORK PIE

Succulent pieces of lean pork with a subtle blend of aromatic spices, encased in crisp pastry – this classic pork pie is delicious. It's perfect for a picnic or a party. And it's a good standby for a quick supper dish too.

Calories per portion: 594   SERVES 8

2 lb/900 g boneless pork
½ level tsp cayenne pepper
1½ level tsp ground ginger
1 level tsp ground mace
1 tbsp freshly chopped parsley
1 tbsp freshly chopped coriander
½ level tsp salt
freshly ground black pepper
5 oz/150 g lard
½ pint/300 ml milk and water
1 lb/450 g plain flour
¼ pint/150 ml stock
1 egg, size 5, beaten
½ oz/15 g gelatine

Preheat oven to Gas 7, 425°F, 220°.

Trim pork, cut into ¼ in/6 mm cubes. Mix with the spices, herbs and the seasoning. Cover and leave on one side while preparing the pastry.

Melt the lard in the milk and water over medium heat. Sift the flour into a large mixing bowl and make a well in the centre. Pour in the lard and mix with a wooden spoon until the flour is fully incorporated. Continue to mix until cool enough to handle then knead until smooth. Cut off a third for the lid and leave covered in the bowl.

Roll out the pastry on a lightly floured surface and use to line a fluted raised pork pie tin or an 8 in/20.5 cm loose-bottomed, round cake tin. Bring sides of the pastry up to top of the tin.

Spoon the prepared pork filling into the pastry-lined tin, packing it down firmly with the back of a spoon. Pour in 3 tbsp of the stock.

Roll out remaining pastry for a lid, reserve trimmings. Brush the top edge of the pie with beaten egg and place lid in position, pressing edges firmly together. Roll out the trimmings and cut out four leaves. Place leaves in position. Brush with egg.

Make a small hole in the centre of the pie to allow the steam to escape.

Place in oven on the centre shelf and cook for 30 mins. Lower temperature to Gas 4, 350°F, 180°C, and cook for a further 1½-2 hrs. Cover the top loosely with foil halfway during cooking.

When cooked, remove and allow to cool. Dissolve gelatine in remaining stock, cool then carefully pour into pie. Leave overnight in fridge.

HANDY TIP

If using a loose-bottomed cake tin: when ready to serve, place tin on a clean can then gently ease cake tin away.

1. Cut pork into ¼ in/6 mm cubes. Place in bowl with herbs and spices

2. Pour the milk and lard into sifted flour and mix with a spoon until cool

3. When cool enough to handle, knead the pastry until it is smooth

4. Mould the hot water crust pastry carefully into the sides of the tin

5. Pack the meat firmly into the tin, making sure there are no air pockets

6. Pour the cooled gelatine stock gradually into pie, allowing liquid to settle

BACON PIE

Whether it's supper or lunch-time, no one will be able to resist a large slice of this tasty bacon pie. With its crisp, light, golden pastry and delicious herby sauce spiced with the tang of chives, it makes a mouthwatering family favourite.

Calories per portion: 522   **SERVES 6**

FOR THE PASTRY:

12 oz/350 g plain flour

pinch of salt

3 oz/75 g butter or margarine

4 oz/100 g lard or white
   vegetable fat

FOR THE FILLING:

8 oz/225 g bacon, derinded

2 oz/50 g butter or margarine

2 oz/50 g plain flour

1¼ pints/750 ml skimmed milk

3 eggs, size 3

salt and freshly ground
   black pepper

2 tbsp freshly chopped parsley

1 tbsp freshly chopped chives

1 egg, size 5, beaten

Preheat the oven to Gas 6, 400°F, 200°C, 15 mins before cooking pie.

Sieve flour and salt into a mixing bowl, cube fats and rub into the flour until the mixture resembles fine breadcrumbs. Bind together with about 4 tbsp of cold water to give a firm but pliable dough. Knead on a lightly floured surface until smooth and free from cracks, then wrap and leave in fridge for 30 mins.

To make the filling, discard any cartilage from bacon, then dice bacon and reserve. Melt fat in pan, stir in flour, cook for 2 mins, remove from the heat, then gradually stir in milk. Return pan to heat and bring to the boil, stirring until thickened. Simmer for 2 mins. Remove from the heat, cover with a sheet of damp greaseproof and allow to cool for 30 mins.

When cool, lightly whisk eggs with seasoning then beat into the cooled sauce together with the reserved bacon, the parsley and chives. Stir until thoroughly mixed.

Roll out just over half of the pastry on to a floured surface and use to line a 2 pint/1.2 litre pie dish. Transfer the prepared filling to the pastry-lined dish. Roll out the remaining pastry to form the lid and dampen edges of pastry with a little water. Place lid in position, press edges firmly together, and pinch to form a decorative pattern around the edge. Roll out the pastry trimmings and cut out leaf-shaped decorations with a small cutter. Brush the top of the pie with the beaten egg and fix pastry decorations in place. Make two small slits in the top of the pie to allow the steam to escape.

Bake in oven for 30 mins, then remove and brush again with the egg. Reduce oven to Gas 4, 350°F, 180°C. Continue to cook for a further 20 mins, or until the pastry is cooked and golden brown.

Serve the pie hot or cold with either freshly cooked vegetables or a large mixed salad.

HANDY TIP

Make pastry as described then scatter the bacon over base. Beat 4 eggs with seasoning and pour over. Cover with lid then cook for 35-45 mins or until golden brown.

1. Sieve the flour and salt into a bowl, cut fats into cubes and add to bowl

2. Using fingertips, rub fat into flour until the mixture resembles breadcrumbs

3. Once the sauce has cooled, beat in the eggs, then bacon, parsley and chives

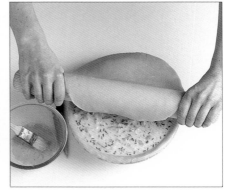

4. Roll out just over half the pastry, then use to line a 2 pint/1.2 litre pie dish

5. Transfer the cooled, prepared bacon filling to the pastry-lined pie dish

6. Roll out remaining pastry to form lid, place on pie, brush with beaten egg

INDEX

ACKNOWLEDGEMENTS

All photography by John Elliott
Except for: Chicken Satay, Plaice Goujons, Fish Terrine and Chicken Gumbo by David Armstrong
Winter Lentil Soup, Onion Tart and Chicken Risotto by Karl Adamson
Smoked Fish Pâté, and Crab Cakes by Ken Field
Bacon Pie by Ferguson Hill

Gina Steer would like to thank Kathryn Hawkins and Jenny Brightman for their help in
assisting in some of the photography, styling and recipe testing.